Reminiscences of a Viennese Psychoanalyst

Sterba in Detroit, ca. 1950.

Reminiscences
of a
Viennese Psychoanalyst

RICHARD F. STERBA, M.D.

WAYNE STATE UNIVERSITY PRESS
DETROIT, 1982

Library of Congress Cataloging in Publication Data

Sterba, Richard.
    Reminiscences of a Viennese psychoanalyst.

    1. Sterba, Richard. 2. Psychoanalysts— Austria— Biography.
3. Psychoanalysis— Austria— History. I. Title. [DNLM: 1. Psychoanalysis—
Austria— Personal narratives. WZ 100 S838]
RC339.52.S73A37 1982   150.19′5′0924 [B]   82-11149
ISBN 0-8143-1716-2

A portion of Chapter 5 appeared in Richard F. Sterba, "Discussions of
Sigmund Freud," *Psychoanalytic Quarterly* 47 (1978): 173-91, and is
included here by permission.

Contents

Preface

A few years ago, at the midwinter meeting of the American Psychoanalytic Association for a historical seminar on psychoanalysis conducted by Dr. Archangelo d'Amore, Dr. d'Amore invited me to give a report on the psychoanalytic community in Vienna as I experienced it. This was the first impetus for me to look back intensely at this period of my life. More recently, a former president of the International Psychoanalytic Association, P. J. Van der Leeuw, published a paper that highlighted the importance of the closely knit group of psychoanalysts formed after World War I around Sigmund Freud in Vienna. The group was active there until the destruction of psychoanalysis in Austria by the Nazis in spring of 1938.

Since Van der Leeuw mentioned my name among these analysts, I felt motivated once more to report on my experiences, observations, and personal opinions during the years 1924 to 1938, when I was a trainee, an active member, and finally a board member of the Vienna Psychoanalytic Society and a member of the faculty of the Vienna Psychoanalytic Institute. Freud himself gave credit to the importance of the Viennese group for his science when he says in the preface to the third charter of *Moses and Monotheism* (Alfred A. Knopf, 1939): "Psychoanalysis, however, which has travelled everywhere during the course of my long life, has not yet found a more serviceable home than in the city where it was born and grew."

I must ask the reader to consider this treatise not as a historical study but as the report of an eyewitness, with all the subjective coloring and misapprehensions that are characteristic of eyewitness reports. However, I assure the reader that I will make every effort to be honest and to present the events recalled as objectively as possible. My main goal is to make it possible for the reader to participate in the atmosphere, the spirit, and the ardent excitement that the direct or indirect contact with Freud stirred in our group. We shared a unique privilege of participating in Freud's discoveries and finding them daily confirmed in the analyses we conducted. We were exhilarated to witness the birth of Freud's new ideas, ideas that were revolutionary even within his own scientific framework, such as the change from the transformation theory of anxiety to the signal significance of this affect, or the change from the concept of the ego as a victim to the concept of the ego as the controller of the id. This influx of ideas stimulated the enthusiastic work and elation so characteristic of our Viennese group in the twenties and thirties.

It would be most gratifying for me if, by this presentation of my memories, I could make it possible for the reader to empathize with our glorious esprit de corps and our envyless admiration for Freud, whom we all recognized as a genius and a unique scientific leader. The indefatigable eagerness with which we devoted ourselves to the "cause," the common pride in participating in the dissemination of Freud's discoveries and theories gave an exhilarating feeling of direct participation in Freud's monumental work. It brought us near his creative genius and his powerful ideas even if we had only indirect contact with his personality. We experienced vivendo what Freud said about the power of such participation: "Men are strong, so long as they represent a powerful idea."*

When I was starting my analysis in the spring of 1924, Freud's scientific edifice had developed from a therapeutic procedure for patients suffering from neuroses to a more general science of the human mind. Freud had already explained the universal human experience of dreams and slip actions. He had investigated the mutual influences of culturalization and repression and had applied psychoanalytic theory and investigative notes to literature, art, and biography. The universal validity of the basic psychoanalytic tenets was thus established. From this

---

*"On the History of the Psychoanalytic Movement," *Standard Edition of the Complete Works of Sigmund Freud* [hereafter *Standard Edition*](London: Hogarth Press, 1958), vol. 14, p. 66.

foundation, psychoanalysis would extend its interest during the next decades. Freud would broaden and change some of the basic early assumptions in his theory which provided a more profound understanding of the human mind. His investigation expanded over the years from the treatment of individual patients to wider areas of human experience, to the human condition in general, and to an investigation of human civilization and its development.

I. Childhood and Education*

My birthplace is Vienna, the former capital of the multinational Austro-Hungarian monarchy. It was also the residence of the Habsburg emperors. In the year of my birth, 1898, Kaiser Franz Josef had ruled the Habsburg empire for fifty years.

The Austro-Hungarian empire was at that time a constitutional monarchy. The form of government was semidemocratic; approval or veto was still a powerful tool in the hand of the emperor. The former ruling class, the aristocracy, had been considerably curtailed in privileges and power, first by the revolution of 1848 and then by the ascendancy of the Liberal party in the sixties. This party represented the growing industry, high finance, commerce, science, and art. The most important party line was the culturalization of the lower strata of the population. Toward the end of the nineteenth century the liberals had already stepped down from the political arena and were yielding their position to three power groups, each led by a strong personality. The most important group was the Christian Socialist party led by Dr. Karl Lueger, called *der schoene* Karl ("handsome Karl"). Lueger was later, for many years, the mayor of Vienna. He was extremely popular with the lower middle class, particularly the artisans and small shopkeepers. The Christian Socialist party was closely connected with the Catholic church, to which the vast majority of the Austrian population belonged. Dr. Lueger and his followers were outspokenly anti-Semitic. The anti-Semitism of the church

*This chapter is actually an addendum on which the publisher insisted after having read the manuscript. The editors thought that readers would like to have more information about the life and education of the author. I yield to their experience with the reading public.

enhanced the hostility toward Jews that was traditional in the mentality of the Viennese petite bourgeoisie.

The second group striving for power was led by the strong-willed and demagogic Georg von Schoenerer. This party stood for German domination in the monarchy and strove for unification of the German part of Austria with the German Reich. Schoenerer and his followers were viciously anti-Semitic. (Many years later, Adolf Hitler nourished his hatred of the Jews with the writings of Schoenerer.) Against the rising danger of anti-Semitism in Austria, Theodor Herzl created the Zionist movement.

In addition to these political groups, a third party was gaining importance under the leadership of Victor Adler. This party represented the working class, but in the beginning of the twentieth century it attracted many progressively minded intellectuals. The orientation of the party was Marxist; it aimed at an evolutionary socialization.

Besides the pressures from these power groups, the monarchy was exposed to the forces of the different nations that wanted either independence or unification with neighboring countries of common or related language. What held the empire together was Kaiser Franz Josef, or, rather, what he represented — the Habsburg empire, a European political power structure of relative stability that had lasted through eight hundred years. When Franz Josef died in 1916, the monarchy fell apart.

I was brought up amidst the struggle of the political forces which undermined the basic structure of the empire. But the waves of the stormy politics hardly reached me during my childhood. Our home was not religious, nor did my father have strong political convictions. Politics were never mentioned in my family.

The provenience of my parents was typical for many Viennese. My paternal grandparents were both Czechs born in Bohemia, at the time one of the crown countries of the monarchy. My grandfather, a tailor by trade, had settled in the province of Upper Austria in a village not far from Salzburg. He came there at the time of the construction of the Western railroad, the *Kaiserin Elisabeth Westbahn*, which led from Vienna through the provinces of Lower and Upper Austria, Salzburg, Tyrol, and Vorarlberg into Switzerland. Railroad building, which had to be done by manual labor, gave jobs to thousands of laborers and occupied a staff of engineers. In turn, their need for clothing did not leave my grandfather idle. Both paternal grandparents died before I was born. My father grew up as a village boy and, like so many people of Czech origin who spent their childhood in the German part of the monarchy, he identified with the Austro-German population.

My grandfather wanted his son to become a tailor also. But my father's outstanding performance in grade school motivated his teacher to urge my grandfather to let the boy enter the gymnasium (boys' secondary school) in Salzburg. In this way my father acquired a humanistic education. After finishing his gymnasium, he studied mathematics and physics at the University of Vienna and finally taught mathematics and physics in Vienna at a lyceum (a girls' school that roughly corresponded in its curriculum to that of the gymnasium for boys).

Under the German nationalistic propaganda of Georg von Schoenerer, my father's ideology became mildly German nationalistic and anti-Semitic, though he was never politically active. He was narrow in his thinking and in many ways peasantlike in his outlook and habits. He was not fond of social contact; visitors in my parents' home felt unwelcome by his reserved attitude, which sometimes mounted to unfriendliness. He felt at home only when he bowled with the local peasants in the village near Salzburg where we spent our long summer vacations. As a father, he was very strict and authoritarian; physical punishment belonged to his educational arsenal. My four-years'-older brother and I were mainly afraid of him and we never developed a close relationship with him in our childhood and youth. He treated his sons without any psychological understanding. Later in life, some of his former pupils became patients of mine and I heard them complain about my father's strictness and lack of empathy with his pupils. But he was respected for being very just in his grading.

It was *de rigueur* that my father's two sons—there were no other children—should acquire the same humanistic education that he had obtained. He was content and even proud when we both studied medicine and became physicians.

My mother's parents were of mixed nationality. Her father

came from a family of weavers who had been forced to leave their homeland—the German-speaking northern part of Bohemia in the Sudeten Mountains—when the introduction of the mechanical loom in the middle of the nineteenth century put them out of work. (The German author and playwright Gerhardt Hauptmann dramatized the plight of these people in his famous revolutionary play *The Weavers*.) My maternal grandfather emigrated to Lodz, a Polish city that then belonged to the Russian empire. There he married a Polish woman who bore him six children. When my mother was a teenager, the family moved to Vienna, where my grandparents eked out a meager existence by running a small restaurant. My mother learned very early the trade of seamstress; she had no opportunity for a higher education. When she married my father, she continued her trade and ran a workshop that made women's dresses. When I was a small child, she sometimes had four girls working in one of the three small rooms of our apartment. She contributed considerably to the family income, which was most welcome to my parsimonious father. Our standard of living was very restricted, which enabled my father to save a great part of his salary as a lyceum professor, only to lose it all with the downfall of the Austrian empire.

My father dominated the domestic scene and the family life was subservient to him. My mother was a very warm and loving person; she was deeply devoted to her family and anxious to do everything to my father's satisfaction. Her loving care of and concern for her two boys compensated for Father's stern and forbidding nature. It was due to her that our home life was relatively harmonious, and, with the exception of the fear of our father, I look back on a relatively peaceful childhood.

Culturally, our home was impoverished. My father's interests were absorbed by higher mathematics and astronomical theory. He glanced through the daily newspaper in the morning before leaving for his school; the free time after he came home from work was devoted to his studies in his special field, if he did not have to grade the tests of his pupils. He very rarely read a book outside his professional field, and our bookcase contained only literature in his specialty. We did not even have the great German classics in our home. I learned reading very early and was eager to read, but had hardly any reading material. A cousin of mine had some of the stories of Jules Verne in German and I devoured them avidly and repeatedly. There was neither a school nor a public library, and my father was not willing to spend money on books if they were not in his field of study. I do not know how I obtained Cooper's Leatherstocking tales in a German translation. They were my favorite reading during grade school.

GYMNASIUM

The first enlargement of my intellectual horizon occurred when I entered the gymnasium. Since I was a good student, I was allowed to skip the fifth grade and I entered the gymnasium a year earlier than most of my classmates, at the age of ten. In order to be admitted, one had to take a written entrance examination to prove that one could write and read in two characters, Gothic and Latin, and that one knew how to spell faultlessly and was accomplished in sentence analysis. In addition, one had to have a thorough command of the four cardinal operations of elementary mathematics. When I entered the gymnasium, a new world opened up for me. I had the good fortune to enter a newly founded gymnasium. It had opened the year before I entered with the lowest grade attended by only eight or ten pupils. The grade I entered had twenty pupils enrolled. Since there were only two grades established when I attended the first grade, not more than thirty students were in the whole school, whereas the long-established gymnasium had hundreds of students. Our professors had time and energy to devote to the few in their care. Some of the professors were very learned men, sincerely interested in providing the students with a classical education. During the first years, we received much individual attention, to our great profit. The diretor of the gymnasium, whose son attended class with me, was young and ambitious as well as strict and exacting. Our professors made most of our studies an interesting and profitable experience.

The importance of the gymnasium for higher education in Europe cannot be overstated. The most important subjects were the classical languages. The curriculum consisted of eight grades that were designated by Latin numbers, starting with *Prima* and ending with *Octava*. (In Germany, the grades were counted in the opposite direction: *Octava* was the lowest, *Prima* the highest.) A pupil of the first grade was called a *Primaner*, a second grader was *Secundaner*, etc. At the end of the eighth grade one had to undergo a week of rigorous written and oral examinations in the main subjects in the presence of the director of the gymnasium and a representative of the government (most gymnasia were government institutions). This ordeal was called *Matura* *(Abitur* in Germany). The examination took place in badly ventilated classrooms early in July, after all of the other grades had started their summer vacations. It was dreaded by all who had to go through it—even Freud, who had been *primus* (top student) in all eight grades of the gymnasium, expressed some apprehension about it in a letter to a friend. Since the professors had had ample opportunity during eight years to judge the students' capabilities and knowledge and to eliminate those who did not come up to the prescribed academic standards, the *Matura*, in my opinion, represented in its torturous features a psychological equivalent of the puberty rites of primitives.* On the evening of the last day of the examinations, after the diplomas had been distributed, the *Maturanten* met with the professors in the private room of a nearby restaurant. They were officially permitted to drink beer and had to listen to a speech by the director, who congratulated them on reaching "maturity" and being qualified to attend the university.

Latin was the backbone of the curriculum at the gymnasium. It was taught for eight years, eight hours per week. The gymnasium was the continuation of the *Lateinschule* (Latin school) of former centuries, the center of higher education for adolescents. We studied classical Greek six hours per week for six years. The student left the gymnasium well acquainted with the classical literary works of antiquity. It still strikes me as peculiar that we were not taught one living language. I had to acquire my knowledge of French and Italian privately. I learned English only when I was thirty years old.

*Cf. Theodor Reik, "Puberty Rites of Savages," in *Ritual Psychoanalytic Studies* (London: Hogarth Press, 1931).

Besides the classical languages, the subjects taught in the gymnasium were German literature, mathematics, physics, history and geography, zoology and botany, and a few elementary facts of chemistry. These studies served as the basis for the student's becoming a member of the elite of the *Gebildeten*. I owe to the gymnasium a great deal of my knowledge of the Greek and Roman culture and my interest in art and literature.

Since the student attended the gymnasium from pre-puberty through early adolescence, he passed these important years under the influence of the great cultures of Greece and Rome. Sigmund Freud has acknowledged in his paper "Zur Psychologie des Gymnasiasten"* what lifelong gains he owed to his studies at the gymnasium. In this article, contributed to a *Festschrift* celebrating the fiftieth anniversary of the foundation of the gymnasium that he had attended, Freud describes the emotional reaction he experienced when by chance he met one of the gymnasium professors in later life:

> As you walked through the streets of Vienna—already a gray-beard, and weighed down by all the cares of family life—you might come unexpectedly on some well-preserved, elderly gentleman and would greet him humbly almost, because you had recognized him as one of your former Gymnasium teachers. . . .
>
> In such moments as these, I used to find the present time seemed to sink into obscurity and the years between ten and eighteen would rise from the corners of my memory, with all their anticipations and errors, their painful transformations and blissful successes—my first glimpses of an extinct civilization (which in my case was to bring me unsurpassed consolation in the struggles of life)—my first contact with the sciences, among which it seemed open to

*"Some Reflections on Schoolboy Psychology," *Standard Edition*, vol. 13, p. 241. The word *Gymnasiast* is poorly translated as "schoolboy." The *Gymnasiast* was not an ordinary schoolboy; he was a budding member of the academic community and was treated as such. He was, at least in the higher grades, addressed not by the *Du* but by the more respectful *Sie* when he was spoken to by the professor. The title "professor" was, in turn, an indication of the high esteem in which the teachers were held.

me to chose to which of them I should dedicate what were no doubt invaluable services.*

Freud's tribute to his studies at the gymnasium, which he attended four decades earlier than I, expresses the same feeling with which I look back on my years at the gymnasium. The gymnasium gave me not only the knowledge of the subjects but, more important, a familiarity with the broader cultural aspects that the ancient languages transmit. Greek I loved for its poetic beauty, but Latin fascinated me by its clarity of expression and the exactitude of its statements in the shortest and most precise possible form. The study of Latin in itself provided training in logical thinking: the mere sentence structure is the result of concentration on the precision of expression in briefest form. In my opinion, the Western world is greatly impoverished by the abolition of Latin from the curricula of higher education. Besides, Latin is the basis of all Romanic modern languages, like Romanian, Italian, Spanish, French, and some of English. It is much easier to learn any of these languages when one knows Latin. In law and medicine, Latin terms are an indispensable part of the professional language; I find it deplorable that lawyers and doctors use these terms without being familiar with their original meaning.

On the other hand, there were serious defects in the curriculum of the gymnasium. There was a complete lack of instruction on current history. We were left uninformed about the political events in the monarchy as well as about international politics. It seems to me that the government did not favor political knowledge for its younger subjects. Strangely enough, neither political nor international events were ever the subject in our private discussions. We had the feeling that these were concerns for adults, under whose protection we felt secure. The national anthem that we had to sing innumerable times assured us "Oesterreich wird ewig stehn" (Austria will stand forever), and we believed in this prediction.

---

*The first paragraph of this quotation is the official translation by James Strachey in the standard edition of Freud's works. In the second part I corrected Strachey's translation so that it corresponds more closely to the meaning of Freud's original German text.

Knowledge of financial matters was also kept from us. The subject of sex was never mentioned at home or in school. Later, in medical school, the famous anatomist Professor Julius Tandler spoke mockingly of the "asexual anatomy of the gymnasium." We were brought up to be both politically and sexually uninformed subjects of the emperor.

At the gymnasium we had school only from 8:00 A.M. to 1:00 P.M. Only once a week did we have more school in the afternoon. This left ample time for extracurricular activities. Homework did not take up much of my time, particularly since I was not a very industrious student. I had no playmates—to my brother I always was an unwelcome rival whose presence he disliked—and social contact with other children was discouraged by my father's attitude toward strangers in the house.

Unfortunately, the gymnasium that I attended was situated in an outer district of the city. My schoolmates came from petty bourgeois families and most of them had no cultural interests beyond the school curriculum. With one exception, they all became Nazis when Hitler came to power, an indication of their narrow mentality. Although most middle-class families lived in crowded tenement houses called *Mietskasernen* (rent barracks), our family had no contact with the neighbor tenants. During the warm seasons I could spent my leisure time on a playground very near our apartment house and play soccer with other boys. The little park had once been the garden of the palace of Prince Kaunitz, the adviser of Empress Maria Theresia. Typical baroque statuary adorned the entrance, and in the front garden of the palace a bronze Nemean lion squirted a little fountain jet out of his maw, which was pulled wide open by the mighty hands of a bronze Hercules. Baroque artworks and Greek mythology were thus part of my childhood ambience.

The gymnasium provided no musical instruction, though we had a weekly singing lesson. The singing lessons in grade school had aroused my interest in a musical instrument. Our first classroom teacher, whom I greatly admired, accompanied our singing on the violin. I cannot judge how good he was as a fiddler, but at any rate I was so impressed by his playing and by the sound of his violin that I asked my mother to let me study the violin. When I was in second grade, she bought me a half-size violin and engaged a music student of the Vienna conservatory to teach me the basic technique. I enjoyed playing the violin so much that I did not have to be forced to practice. During the following years I developed some proficiency at the violin. My talent for musical expression later gained me acceptance as a pupil by a series of prominent teachers, such as Ottokar Sevčik, Rudolf Kolisch, and Adolf Busch. In the major churches in Austria, the high mass was celebrated with orchestral and choir music. During my years at the gymnasium, I played in the first violin section at the high mass at San Carlo Borromeo, the Karls Kirche, the architectural masterwork of Austria's greatest Baroque architect, Fischer von Erlach. I was therefore exempt from the early mass that the other pupils of the gymnasium had to attend at a local church, while I had to be in church only at eleven. Furthermore, violin playing brought me in contact with families of wider cultural interests than my home and school situation provided. In the beginning of this century, that is, before the gramophone became accepted as a provider of musical experience, the amateur musician was a welcome guest at social gatherings, so I was often invited into circles that would not have been accessible to me without my musical contributions.

MILITARY SERVICE

I was still a student at the gymnasium when the First World War broke out, in August 1914. It caused a radical change in the lives and mentality of the whole population. The declaration of war, first on Serbia, then on Russia, France, and England, was greeted with an unbelievable, almost fanatic enthusiasm that was upheld by the initial victories of the Central Powers. But the stalemate to trench warfare at the different theaters of the war, increasing food shortages, and rationing made the people realize that the expectation of a quick victorious ending of the war by Christmas had to be given up, and the spirit of patriotic frenzy gradually subsided. When, in the spring of 1915, Italy declared war on Austria, the spirit was further dampened and gradually replaced by depression and hopelessness. Austrians began to feel as if they were enclosed in a besieged fortress with dwindling supplies. When I had to join the army in May 1916, shortly before my eighteenth birthday, I—along with most of the draftees—was more concerned with survival than with sacrificing my life for "God, Kaiser, and fatherland." I expected my intellectual and artistic interests to be buried under the commonness and vulgarity of military life and the misery and deadly danger in combat. However, the two and a half years that I spent in the army were not lost for my cultural and artistic development.

When I entered the service, I was assigned to a special group of recruits who were selected to become officers. We were all graduates of the gymnasium. After basic training we were transferred to an officers' school situated at the Hungarian border, one hour's train ride from Vienna. It was there that I became aware of the existence of Freud and psychoanalysis. Strange as it may seem in retrospect, neither in the curriculum at the gymnasium nor outside of it had I ever heard of Freud and his discoveries. In the military wasteland of the barracks and exercising grounds I discovered psychoanalysis. Among my comrades there were some older men who had until then been considered unfit for military service. They had been drafted because the losses in combat were being filled by the very young men hardly of military age, to which group I belonged, or by men beyond military age. Among these men in their forties were some who formed a small group based on their common interests and values. They were what one called *gebildete* intellectuals. Two were writers of considerable reputation, one was a university professor, another was a well-known stage director, and one a composer. I felt drawn to these men because of my intellectual interests and I was included in their discussions, though primarily as a listener. One of these intellectuals was the son of Victor Adler, the founder of Austria's Socialist Democratic party. The Adlers had once occupied the apartment at Berggasse 19 before Freud established himself there. In young Adler's discussions, Sigmund Freud and his psychoanalytic theories were mentioned. These conversations stimulated me to read some of Freud's works.

The first works of Freud's that I read were the five lectures that he gave in 1909 at Clark University, in Worcester, Massachusetts. They are an excellent introduction to psychoanalysis. I remember that I started the little booklet on a long streetcar ride in Vienna while on a leave of absence from the officers' school. I finished it the same evening on the train ride back to the school. What attracted me most was Freud's literary style and his unusually clear and beautiful way of expressing his ideas. Next I read the analysis of a case of hysteria, in which I found that Freud's descriptions of personalities and human feelings and relationships were equal to those of the great writers. Thus, the first image that I obtained of Freud was formed more from the artistic quality of his writings than from their content. Unfortunately, I was soon transferred to a Ukrainian regiment and continued my training at a camp deep inside Hungary. The hardship of drill and exhausting maneuvers left no time and energy for intellectual activity. Upon graduating from the officers' program, I was sent to join my regiment in the Ukraine, and from there I was shipped into combat in a mountainous sector of the Austro-Italian border. I spent several months there and participated in several battles at the Isonzo River under miserable conditions and in continuous mortal danger. The hardships and the malnutrition undermined my health to such a degree that I became sick and had to leave the combat zone. After a short stay at the medical station, I was put on a hospital train and, after some circuitous traveling through Hungary, landed in a war hospital in Vienna.

I managed to stay in the hospital for seven months, although I had recovered my health in a few weeks. It happened that the priest who served at the hospital chapel was eager to have the high mass on Sunday celebrated with music. A conductor who was among the patients of the hospital found enough musicians among the patients to form a choir and an orchestra. The prolongation of my hospital stay I owe to my violin playing. The priest used his influence to keep me and another violinist at the hospital for the longest possible time. This period I could use for cultural development. I had no obligations, and had plenty of time to read, to visit the museums of Vienna, to practice the violin, and to play string quartets with a group of musicians in the hospital.

For bravery in combat I had been prematurely promoted to the rank of lieutenant while still in the hospital. This opened a rich musical experience for me. Half of the standing room on the main floor of the court opera was reserved for military officers for a minimal price. Since the opera had daily performances for ten months of the year, I took this opportunity to attend numerous operas during that season. This and the symphony concerts that I attended alternatingly with the opera made me familiar with many major works of classical and romantic music.

After I had been at the hospital for seven months, the priest could no longer ward off the demands of the military authorities to end my hospitalization. However, I managed to obtain a leave of absence of four months before returning to my regiment in the Ukraine. These four months, the spring and early summer of 1918, I spent in Salzburg, devoting my time to the study of art history and the reading of the German classics and Romanticists. I also continued reading Freud: the introductory lectures, notes on obsessional neurosis, and the interpretation of dreams. I tried to analyze my own dreams, but had to recognize the limitation of self-analysis.

Because of the war, Salzburg was completely devoid of tourists. I could absorb its unique beauty in splendid isolation. It was then that I acquired the enthusiasm for Gothic art which resulted in my first psychoanalytic publication. I will report on this in a later chapter.

In early September 1918, after I returned to my Ukrainian regiment in Stryi, far in the east of the monarchy, it was already obvious that the war was lost. More and more cadres of the army disintegrated, until, early in November 1918, I saw no reason to stay at my command post any longer. I was fortunate to catch the last train to Vienna, where I arrived just a week before armistice was declared. I had already decided to study medicine and I enrolled as a student at the medical school of the Vienna University. Time and the experiences of two and a half years in the army had matured me. I studied diligently and was awarded one of the rare scholarships.

The living conditions in postwar Vienna were miserable. The official food rations were so small that one had to supplement them at the black market in order to survive. It took five years after the end of the war for the first *Schlagobers*, whipped cream, so essential to Austrians, to appear in the *"Kaffee Houses."* At home and at the university there was no fuel for heating and the apartments and classrooms were bitter cold. The temperature in the dissection room was 0° C.; we and the professor developed frostbite on our hands. I assume that the blanket on Freud's couch, which is visible in so many photographs of Freud's office, was a remnant and reminder of the chilly ambience in which analysis had to thrive.

EDITHA

In the winter of 1923, I met my future wife, Editha von Radanowicz-Hartmann. She was finishing her studies at the University of Vienna and working as a secretary-typist for Otto Rank, who dictated to her the manuscript of *An Analysis of a Neurosis in Dreams* (1926) and *The Trauma of Birth* (1924). Editha's ancestry was even more multinational than mine. Her father was of Croatian stock. Among her mother's ascendants were Germans, Poles, Swiss, and English; one of her eight great-grandmothers was Jewish, which her family considered a "skeleton in the closet."

Editha had her first education at the Sacre Coeur in Prague, where her father occupied a high command post in the Austrian army. When her father went into retirement, the family moved to Baden, a spa near Vienna. Although the humanistic gymnasium in Baden was only for boys, Editha insisted on obtaining a humanistic education. Through his connections with the top government officials, her father obtained for Editha special permission to attend this gymnasium as the only girl among more than three hundred male students; she finished it in 1918 and enrolled at the University of Vienna, where she studied psychology and musicology. She began her psychoanalytic training in 1925. She and I were among the first trainees; she graduated in 1927. She had studied the piano and was an accomplished pianist when we met.

Through her connection with Otto Rank, Editha obtained the position of editor at the Psychoanalytic Publishing House, which had been established in 1918. She worked there from 1922 until 1932. Editha prepared, with A. J. Storfer, Otto Rank, and Anna Freud, the *Gesammelte Schriften* (the edition of the *Collected*

Works published in 1926 for Freud's seventieth birthday), and on a special edition of *Imago* that was also published on 6 May 1926, in honor of Freud's seventieth birthday and that contained articles by Hans Sachs, Ludwig Jekels, Edward Hitschmann, Melanie Klein, Helene Deutsch, Alfred Winterstein, and Theodor Reik among its twenty-nine contributions.

In spring of 1924, Editha invited me to spend the holidays with her family in Gmunden on Lake Traunsee, not far from Salzburg. I had always heard people raving about the beautiful lakes of the Salzkammergut (which gets its name from its salt mines) and had read about them in Freud's case history of "little Hans," but I had never visited this region. When Editha's maternal grandfather, who had been a four-star general in the Austrian army, retired, he bought an estate on Lake Traunsee, situated within walking distance of the town of Gmunden. On the maternal side, Editha's family was of old nobility; her father was ennobled upon his retirement. In 1914, Editha's parents moved to Gmunden and lived on the estate. The house had originally been built in the seventeenth century by the bishops of Passau as a stone hunting lodge and had been enlarged by Editha's grandfather. It was situated sixty feet above the lake, and the view over the lake, framed by the foothills and higher peaks of the alpine range, was magnificent. The house had enough rooms for a large family and was filled with antique furniture. As long as we lived in Austria, we spent our vacations and extended holidays there. During the five to six weeks of our summer vacation, some of our foreign patients spent time in Gmunden, which was a well-known summer resort, so that they could continue their analyses. From Gmunden we often availed ourselves of the famous Salzburg music festivals during the summer months.

II. Introduction to and Education in Psychoanalysis, 1923-1926

As a medical student at the University of Vienna in the early 1920s, my awareness of psychoanalysis increased. The professor ordinarious of psychiatry and head of the department at the university was then Wagner von Jauregg, who had won the Nobel Prize for his discovery of malaria therapy for general pareses. His orientation was predominantly organic, and when he mentioned psychoanalysis it was only to make a more or less sarcastic remark—or, as he put it, a good-natured joke—about it. He obviously did not believe in it enough to present it to students as a serious matter. Most of the senior members of the psychiatric faculty were openly hostile when they mentioned analysis in their lectures; I had the impression that they felt threatened by Freud, who was then a revolutionary in the psychiatric establishment. However, one of Von Jauregg's assistants, Paul Schilder, taught psychoanalytic concepts and demonstrated their validity with clinical material. Schilder was a man of renown in the field of psychiatry. His evening lectures greatly stimulated me toward further study. Sigmund Freud had already become world famous. The educated world could no longer ignore Freud's discoveries and ideas, and in the early twenties they were the subject of heated controversy, which stirred my interest even more to read Freud's works and other contributions to the psychoanalytic literature. I was particularly fascinated by the writings on applied psychoanalysis by Freud, Otto Rank, Hans Sachs, and others who contributed to *Imago*, the periodical on applied psychoanalysis. They satisfied my interest in psychology as well as my interest in art and literature. Soon I realized that a psychological knowledge in depth was accessible only to somebody who had explored the unconscious through the application of the analytic method with patients, an insight that became for me an important motive to become a psychoanalyst.

When I graduated from medical school in October 1923, I took a position at one of the urban hospitals on the outskirts of the city, the Wilhelminenspital. My job provided a minimal income and left me enough time to pursue my goal of becoming an analyst. I heard that there was a psychoanalytic ambulatorium (outpatient clinic) in the section of Vienna where the university hospitals were located. It held office hours two evenings a week. (In German, the word *Klinik* signifies a hospital for inpatients. The term is derived from the Greek word *klinein*, which means "lying down." What in English is called "clinic" is in German designated as *Ambulatorium*, which is derived from the Latin *ambulare*, "to walk around.")

One evening in December 1923, I went to the ambulatorium to inquire about becoming an analyst. I was seen by an elderly physician whose name was Eduard Hitschmann. I told him that I wanted to become an analyst and he explained to me that I would have to undergo a personal analysis. When I said that my meager salary at the hospital made it impossible for me to pay for analysis, he replied that I would have to wait until a member of the society had an opening for a student. He then asked me a few questions about myself. The interview was cursory, lasting no longer than twenty minutes. Hitschmann dismissed me by telling me that I would have to wait for further notice. I left with the feeling that I did not have much of a chance. Hitschmann had been reserved and distant. I had the impression that he did not think much of me and that I should not expect much success. I had had no recommendation, since I was not acquainted with anybody in the psychoanalytic community at that time who could have furthered my intention to learn psychoanalytic therapy. After my brief meeting with Hitschmann, I thought I might have to give up my desire to enter the new field. However, my interest remained undiminished.

At one of Paul Schilder's lectures, I learned that the Vienna Psychoanalytic Society was arranging a series of introductory lectures for the general public in order to arouse a wider interest in psychoanalysis. I welcomed the opportunity to learn more about the new science and to get to know some of the people who were active in it.

The first evening session of this series was conducted early in 1924 by A. J. Storfer. Storfer was at that time the director of the Psychoanalytic Publishing House. He had no medical degree, but had participated in the research activity at Burghoelzli, near Zurich, the leading psychiatric institution in Switzerland, headed then by Professor Eugen Bleuler and his close collaborator, C. G. Jung. These two outstanding psychiatrists had become aware of the importance of Freud's discoveries. Storfer had taken part in the "association" experiments that Jung had conducted at Burghoelzli during the first decade of this century. The experiments demonstrated the strict determination of what was called *freier Einfall*, poorly translated as "free association." (The German word *Einfall*, which literally means "falling in," describes so well the sensation experienced when a valid thought is produced in connection with a given psychic element. Such an *Einfall* enters the consciousness as if it were falling in from outside.) Often the *freie Einfall* at first seems unconnected with the presented element and then is met with astonishment and surprise by the person who produces it. By thorough examination, one discovers that the *Einfall* is in a meaningful, though often roundabout, way connected with the conscious content to which it is produced. It is determined by unconscious forces and can be used for the recognition of unconscious contents and motivations.

Storfer's introductory lecture was attended by approximately thirty persons; among them was Dr. Hitschmann. When Storfer asked for a volunteer from the audience for a demonstration of the association experiment, I expressed my willingness. The subject to which I was to associate was a reproduction of a painting by the Swiss painter Ferdinand Hodler. I had seen the original at a Hodler exhibition in Bern, Switzerland. I remember that the painting presented a series of human figures in a rituallike dance. First somewhat haltingly, then more assuredly, I verbalized my associations with the details of the picture. When Storfer asked me to associate a second time, I deviated at some points. I could recognize that the deviations were determined by an emotional experience that I had had on my visit to Bern, and I explained some of it to the audience. Storfer seemed pleased with my performance. The experiment took about half an hour. Storfer used my association to demonstrate the validity of the principle of psychic determinism, which is so basic in psychoanalysis.

After the lecture ended, Dr. Hitschmann met me at the exit of the lecture room and addressed me in a very positive way: "You have shown that you are very intelligent." My performance must have impressed him, for a few weeks later I received a postcard from him advising me that I could begin analysis with him on a certain day of the following week. I started my analysis in the early spring of 1924. Since I did not have any money—the salary from the hospital was just sufficient to provide a bare existence—I was not charged for my analysis. However, it was expected that in the future I would conduct the treatment of some patients from the ambulatorium gratuitously or for a minimal contribution to be paid to the ambulatorium.

Karl Abraham and Max Eitingon, at that time the leading personalities in the analytic field in Berlin, had founded the first official training institute in Berlin in 1920. Four years later, the Vienna Psychoanalytic Institute was established, under the directorship of Helene Deutsch. However, the official series of lectures and seminars was not inaugurated until January 1925. Before 1925 no organized training was available in Vienna. Originally, Freud had thought that self-analysis, mainly the analysis of one's own dreams, combined with the study of the psychoanalytic literature, prepared one sufficiently for the task of doing psychoanalytic therapy of neurotic patients. He had not realized that self-analysis was possible only for a genius like himself and that ordinary persons, even those with a considerable gift for insight, needed the help of an experienced analyst to explore their unconscious. Only at the congress in Budapest in 1918 did Freud and Hermann Nunberg propose that one had to undergo a thorough analysis with an experienced colleague in order to be prepared for doing analytic work. Since then, personal analysis has become the most important part of psychoanalytic training.

Before the establishment of the institute, there existed only two official activities of the Vienna Psychoanalytic Society: the scientific meetings of the society, and the operation of the psychoanalytic ambulatorium, which had functioned since its establishment in 1922 as a diagnostic and referral center. The meetings of the society were a continuation of those of the *psychologische Mittwochgesellschaft* (Psychological Wednesday Society), an informal gathering of Freud's followers who had met on Wednesday evenings in Freud's apartment since 1902. Between 1908 and 1910, the Wednesday Society developed into the Vienna Psychoanalytic Society because the participants became so numerous that the meetings had to be moved out of Freud's study.

At the same time, a new branch of internal medicine was developed that specialized in the research and therapy of diseases of the heart. I later befriended one of the first internists who practiced in Vienna the specialty devoted to heart diseases. When we met in the late twenties he was a wise old gentleman, still in practice as a heart specialist. His name was Herz (heart); he was perhaps another example of the determining power of names, about which Karl Abraham had written a very convincing paper.

The members of the fast-growing group of heart specialists established an institution for heart research called *Herzstation* (heart station). It was housed in a former private home in the vicinity of the university hospitals. Among the internists who worked there was Dozent* Felix Deutsch. He was the husband of Helene Deutsch, who had been in analysis with Freud and became one of the leading personalities in the Vienna psychoanalytic community. Felix Deutsch arranged for space for the meetings of the Psychoanalytic Society and the activities of the psychoanalytic ambulatorium at the heart institute. Since the staff of the *Herzstation* worked only in the morning, the building was unoccupied during the afternoon and evening. On the second floor of the two-story building was a lecture room with a centrally located rectangular conference table. Approximately eighteen persons could sit around the table; there were more chairs along the walls of the room. At the time I joined the group, this accommodation was sufficient for the meetings of the society, which had only forty-two members and of these not all attended meetings regularly. In general, not more than twenty-five to thirty people were present. The ventilation of the room was poor and the smoking, in which most members indulged vigorously, made breathing difficult toward the end of each meeting. One of the

*Dozent is the equivalent of assistant professor in United States.

nonsmokers who suffered from the increasing clouds of smoke that filled the room was Anna Freud. Her eyes began to smart badly, but nobody had pity on nonsmokers at that time.

The president of the society was Sigmund Freud. However, at the time I joined the analytic group, Freud had already had the cancer operation that took place in 1923, and was suffering from the aftereffects. The operation had consisted of a resection of the larger part of the right upper jawbone. Because of the suffering and torment that the operational scarring and the construction of a prosthesis caused him, Freud was unable to attend the scientific meetings of the society. It took a long time before a prosthesis was constructed that fit properly and enabled Freud to speak relatively unhampered and to attend some meetings.

Dr. Paul Federn, one of the earliest of Freud's followers, chaired the meetings in his function as vice-president after 1925. Before that, Otto Rank had chaired the meetings. There were two groups of active members. The old guard were Otto Rank, Paul Federn, Joseph Friedjung, Eduard Hitschmann, Ludwig Jekels, Helene and Felix Deutsch, Robert Hans Jokl, Richard Nepallek, Hermann Nunberg, Theodor Reik, Isidor Sadger, Paul Schilder, Maxim Steiner, Dr. Hug-Hellmuth, Dr. Karl Weiss, A. J. Storfer, Alfred Winterstein, and Siegfried Bernfeld. Five of these (Bernfeld, Reik, Storfer, Rank, and Winterstein) were nonphysicians. Most had had no or only rudimentary personal analysis. The second group of active members were younger. Most had joined the analytic group during the early twenties. Each of them had had personal analysis. Among them were Anna Freud, Wilhelm Reich, Edward Bibring, Heinz Hartmann, Wilhelm Hoffer, Otto Isakower, Robert Waelder, Jenny Pollak, René Spitz, Otto Fenichel, and Jeanne Lampl de Groot.

This younger group had privately founded a seminar of their own which served as a forum for the exchange of theoretical ideas, discussion of clinical and therapeutic subjects, and the discussion of analytic literature in a less inhibited atmosphere than in the presence of the older members. Since the participants of this seminar were all considerably younger than the prewar members of the society, it was called the Kinderseminar (childrens' seminar). It was not and never became an official subgroup of the society, but it remained active as a study group of the younger members during the second and third decades of this century. Before I started my personal analysis, I had attended some of the meetings, which took place once a month in the home of one of the participants. When I talked about these meetings at the beginning of my analysis, Dr. Hitschmann forbade me to attend the Kinderseminar, whereas he still permitted me to attend the International Congress of Psychoanalysis, which took place in spring of 1924 in Salzburg.

The strictness with which Dr. Hitschmann forbade me to attend the private meetings of the younger members gave me the impression that some of the older members were jealous of the eagerness of the younger members to further their analytic growth and knowledge. Whereas some members of the establishment (Helene Deutsch and Hermann Nunberg) often attended the Kinderseminar, Dr. Hitschmann never came to these meetings. The flourishing of the unofficial Kinderseminar confirmed the need for an official training curriculum after the model of the Berlin Institute for Psychoanalysis.

I was thrilled to attend the meeting of the International Psychoanalytic Association in Salzburg in April 1924. It was my first big event in the field of my vocation and it gave me the opportunity to meet or at least to see many of the important personalities with whose writings I had then become familiar. As far as I remember, all papers were read in German; some of the contents were too advanced for a neophyte to absorb. I was most impressed by Karl Abraham, who presented his paper "Beitraege der Oralerotik zur Charakterbildung" (Contributions of oral eroticism to character formation). I also remember that Helene Deutsch spoke about "The Psychology of the Female in the Functions of Procreation." One afternoon session was devoted to a discussion of the relationship of psychoanalytic theory to psychoanalytic technique. Although I was not able to follow the presentation and discussion with complete understanding, I remember Franz Alexander's contribution. He spoke on the metapsychology of the psychoanalytic process of healing. More than by Alexander's paper I was impressed by the charming informality with which Sandor Ferenczi discussed the paper. A paper by Wilhelm Reich, "The Therapeutic Significance of the Genital Libido," which he presented in a forceful manner, left me with an impression more of the power of the speaker than of the content. Ernest Jones introduced a discussion on the relationship of psychoanalytic theory to psychoanalytic technique, a discussion that I was not knowledgeable enough to comprehend. What I felt very much was the spirit that dominated the members of the congress. Their number was not more than seventy in my estimation, but they were full of pioneer spirit and enthusiastically devoted to the cause. To observe their attitude enhanced my desire to become fully one of the carriers of Freud's discoveries and their application in therapy. The atmosphere of the congress made me feel that I was witness to and participant in a cause that would be of tremendous consequences for the whole of mankind once it was generally recognized and became influential in all fields of human study.

Besides the society meetings, the other official function of the society was the operation of the psychoanalytic ambulatorium under the direction of Dr. Eduard Hitschmann. He was assisted by Dr. Wilhelm Reich. The ambulatorium had no funds. It was started as a diagnostic and referral center; the intention of its founders was to make analysis accessible to people who did not have the means to pay for private treatment. The Psychoanalytic Society had established the rule that every active member had the obligation to treat two patients for a minimal fee. Suitable cases were selected by the staff of the ambulatorium. The members had the right to absolve themselves from this obligation by giving a monthly contribution to the ambulatorium. If my memory serves me correctly, the ransom amounted to 100 schillings per month, which at that time corresponded roughly to $25.00. From 1926 on this money was used for the salary of some younger analysts who were paid as employees of the ambulatorium. Grete Bibring, Dr. Eduard Kronengold (Kronold), and I were, after Wilhelm Reich, the first salaried therapists employed by the ambulatorium.

In the midtwenties, the society members thought it necessary to promote the cause of psychoanalysis in wider public circles. A "propaganda committee" was founded for this purpose. (The German word *propaganda* means "publicity" and does not have the pejorative connotation that the English "propaganda" carries.) The series of public lectures that I had attended were part of this public relations effort. The interest of the public was indeed stimulated, to the extent that the city of Vienna gave the society a building site at the lower end of the Berggasse for the construction of a building that would house the society and the ambulatorium. However, the money for the building could not be raised and the plan had to be dropped.

Paul Federn and Heinrich Meng edited a psychonalytic *Volksbuch,* a book with popular presentations of psychoanalytic subjects. The establishment of the bimonthly publication for psychoanalytic pedagogy was an additional effort to widen the interest in psychoanalysis among teachers and parents. This was one of the periodicals published by the Psychoanalytic Publishing House. All the productive members contributed to it and it was widely read. My introduction to the psychoanalytic theory of the libido appeared there in 1932.

At that time, some unsolicited publicity for psychoanalytic therapy brought an influx of patients to the ambulatorium. A weekly magazine called *Bettauer's Wochenschrift* began publication in Vienna. Josef Bettauer, the editor, was an Austrian who had spent some years in New York working as a journalist. He was also the author of a series of popular novels. In his new weekly, he openly discussed sexuality in its different forms. This led to a court action against him, in which he was acquitted. *Bettauer's Wochenschrift* was very liberal in its content; it editorialized in favor of psychoanalytic therapy. One part of the magazine was devoted specifically to answering questions concerning sexual matters and frequently recommended to questioners who had sexual problems to seek help at the psychoanalytic ambulatorium. This brought more people to the center than could be treated. In March 1926, Josef Bettauer was shot and killed by a fanatic Nazi. His *Wochenschrift* ceased to be published.

Most people who came to the ambulatorium through *Bettauer's Wochenschrift* were unsophisticated and uninformed in psychological matters. Their naiveté was an advantage for their analytic treatment, because they could not have used superficial and poorly understood psychoanalytic concepts to resist their therapy.

When I started my personal analysis in the spring of 1924, I was still a resident at the hospital in the outskirts of the city. The service was not very time consuming, so I could devote myself to the study of the psychoanalytic literature. My personal analysis and the acquaintance with analytic findings soon sharpened my observational faculty for psychodynamic manifestations. Two particular observations stand out in my mind. At the outpatient clinic for children it occurred repeatedly that when a small boy had to lie down naked on the examination table, he covered his penis with both hands and anxiously begged "Don't cut it off." Needless to say, he received comforting assurance. This was a most impressive manifestation of castration anxiety, which we find omnipresent and ubiquitously troubling in the analyses of men.

The second observation took place on the children's ward, where nuns were functioning as nurses. These nuns, in their sexually frustrating condition, were extremely sensitive to all activities of children which they might suspect were disguised masturbation. They chased the children off the rocking horse when they rocked excitedly and when a little girl sat down on a big rubber ball, she was shouted at: "Get off of that ball right away, you nasty child." Thus, I learned by direct observation how, with these nuns, the increase of the drive intensity due to frustration intensifies the defense.

The institute was then still only in the planning stage. When I had been in analysis for six months, Dr. Hitschmann suggested that I take my first patient for treatment. At that time, beginners started very early to treat their first, then soon a second analytic case. The cases were chosen from the multitude of applicants for therapy at the ambulatorium. For the first two years I had to see my patients in my room in my parents' apartment because I had no office.

My first supervisor was Dr. Robert Jokl. Although he was a member of the society, he had an extensive neurological practice; my impression was that he had limited experience as an analyst. During my supervisory sessions in his office, he always had the water boiling in a kettle where he sterilized his syringes.

My first patient was a young man who suffered from what we called *Befangenheitsneurose,* characterized by bashfulness and a tendency to blush that severely inhibited him in his social contact. I soon recognized the underlying strong homosexual trends of the patient; however, I did not deal with them until they expressed themselves almost explosively in the transference. One day in the second month of his treatment, the patient brought an oil painting, which he wanted me to accept as a present. It was rather large, approximately three feet by five feet; he told me that he had bought it for me. It presented a naked nymph chased in the woods by an equally naked satyr. I was bewildered by this sudden onslaught of acting out of the transference. Not knowing what to do, I asked the patient for associations to the picture, which made him very uncomfortable. At the end of the session, he left the picture in the room. In my bewilderment I turned for help to my supervisor. I telephoned Jokl from the nearest pay station to tell him about the episode. He advised me to give the picture back to the patient in the next session and to analyze the patient's action ruthlessly. In the next session with the patient I followed Jokl's advice. The patient listened for a short time, then got up from the couch, took the picture, which was still standing where he had put it the day before, and left the session; I never heard from him again. I had to recognize that following my supervisor's advice had turned my first attempt as a psychoanalytic therapist into a failure.*

At the same time that I began to see my first patient, in the fall of 1924, I started to attend the society meetings and the technical seminars that Wilhelm Reich had begun in 1922. Reich had the greatest influence on my development as a psychoanalytic therapist. He was an impressive personality full of youthful intensity. His manner of speaking was forceful; he expressed himself well and decisively. He had an unusual flair for psychic dynamics. His clinical astuteness and technical skill made him an excellent teacher and his technical seminar was so instructive that many of the older members of the society attended it regularly. In the seminar, one of the members of the society (at a later stage, usually one of the trainees of the institute) reported on a

---

*"Rücksichtslos analysieren." After reading this manuscript, Dr. Hans Lobner drew my attention to the fact that a case of erythrophobia (Beangenheitsneurose) had been discussed in the technical seminar a year before I was given this case for treatment. The discussion in the seminar pointed out the homosexual component in such cases, their tendency to paranoia, and that erythrophobia and schizophrenia have much in common. I find it peculiar that after this discussion an erythrophobic was given to a beginner as the first case.

case he had in analytic treatment. Reich was particularly brilliant in his synopsis of the report, which he organized according to his excellent understanding of the dynamics of the presented material. His technical advice to the person who reported gave me the basic understanding of the handling of transference and of resistances.

Reich had a particular sensitivity for the recognition of latent resistances and their often hardly noticeable influence on the patient's conscious material. The form in which the patient brought forth his material, his manner and his peculiarity of speech, how he entered the office, how he shook hands with the analyst (in Vienna an established custom at the beginning and closing of each session)—all this Reich taught us to use as important information, particularly about latent resistances. We students and younger members of the group gained tremendously from his insight into and technique in handling resistances. My first supervisor, and with him quite a few of the older members, had not developed the skill of dealing with resistances, particularly transference resistances, and often still tried to overcome them with a direct (that is, nonanalytic) approach. Many of Reich's technical rules, particularly his advice to interpret resistance first from the ego side and only later from the id side became common practice in analytic treatment. Reich published several papers containing material from the seminars on the technical approach to resistances, culminating in his last psychoanalytic book, *Character Analysis* (1929). This book serves even today as an excellent introduction to psychoanalytic technique. In my opinion, Reich's understanding of and technical approach to resistances prepared the way for Anna Freud's *Ego and the Mechanisms of Defense* (1936).

Reich's seminar was of such clinical and technical value and was such an excellent learning experience for young and old that occasionally even a member of the older group found it instructive to present for the trainees a continuous report on a case in treatment. I remember one event somewhat later in Reich's seminar which illustrates Reich's clinical acumen and psychodynamic foresight. I think it was in 1927 or 1928 that Helene Deutsch reported on a case of a young girl with whom she had just begun analytic treatment. What I have preserved in my mind is that after Helene Deutsch's second or third report, some younger participants talked to Reich after the case presentation. He showed us what he had written in his notebook during Helene Deutsch's report: *"Wird durchgehen"* (i.e., she will leave treatment). And, in fact, at the following seminar, Helene Deutsch reported that the patient had quit treatment. This incident fortified our confidence in Reich's psychodynamic insight.

In January 1925, the training institute of the Vienna Psychoanalytic Society officially opened. The first class consisted of approximately fifteen students, including Grete Bibring, Eduard Kronold, my future wife, Editha, some American and Dutch students, and me; half of the class had medical degrees. The director of the institute was Helene Deutsch; Siegfried Bernfeld was vice-president and Anna Freud was secretary. The program of lectures and seminars presented by the institute was very rich and was given by the best minds in the field in Vienna. The lectures were given at the Herzstation. Siegfried Bernfeld opened the series with ten lectures entitled "What Is Psychoanalysis: An Introductory Lecture Course for Physicians and Laypersons." I attended all ten lectures and was very much taken by Bernfeld's presentation and personality. He was a fascinating speaker with a remarkable facility of verbal expression. Even his appearance was impressive. He was tall and gaunt, with deeply set, dark, penetrating eyes. There was something demonic in his expressiveness; he knew how to rivet your attention to what he had to say. I always admired his brilliant mind and the Savonarola-like power with which he held the audience's attention.

Hermann Nunberg held a series of seminars in which Freud's *Three Contributions to the Theory of Sex* and *The Ego and the Id* were studied and discussed. Paul Federn conducted a ten-session seminar on elements of psychoanalytic technique. I attended Theodor Reik's ten lectures on unconscious feelings of guilt. Paul Schilder lectured ten evenings on psychoanalysis in psychiatry, Robert Waelder spoke eight times on the logical structure of psychoanalysis. Eduard Hitschmann gave five lectures on psychic impotence and its treatment. Because many of the trainees and all of the teachers worked during the day, these lectures and seminars were always given in the evening. My evenings were fully occupied with learning and absorbing the wealth of information. Even later, when I was already a member of the society, most of the evenings were given to listening to or giving lectures and attending or conducting seminars. I remember Anna Freud saying in one of the late meetings: "Sleep, what is that?" But the absorption, discussion, and application of Freud's powerful ideas enabled us to carry on with unabating fervor.

From January of 1925 on, I attended as many of the lectures and seminars officially offered by the institute as my service as resident at the hospital permitted. Most of my weekday evenings were occupied by attending the curriculum. The work with the analytic patients, who were seen five times per week, and the supervision took up the rest of my free time. The most instructive part of the curriculum for me remained the biweekly seminar of continuous case presentations conducted by Wilhelm Reich. This and the society meetings were the most important events of the week.

I had attended Wilhelm Reich's technical seminar and had received a first orientation in analytic technique when I started my second case. I treated him for several months without supervision because my analyst thought that I should try this apparently simple neurosis without help. Since this case played an important role in my early training, I will report on him more in extenso.

The patient, a twenty-year-old male, had sought help at the ambulatorium because of sexual difficulties and a very embarrassing symptom. The patient lived in his parents' home. He had a steady girlfriend with whom he had had normal sexual relations until a traumatic experience greatly disturbed him. It so happened that a young female relative of the family stayed at his parents' home for a few days. She was making advances to the attractive young man and seduced him. After she had left, he found that he had acquired scabies, a minor venereal infection, through the sexual contact. The ointment with which he was treated by his physician caused an ulceration on the remnants of his foreskin, which became secondarily infected. The lymph glands in his groin became swollen and painful and he had to stay in bed and be treated with hot compresses, which his mother applied. He was cured in two weeks and wanted to resume the sexual activity with his girlfriend. But, to his dismay, he was unable to have an erection. This caused him great embarrassment and worry. At the same time, he developed a very disturbing hysterical symptom. When he was in public places where he had to take off his hat, such as in a restaurant or a cafe, he had the feeling that his hair was standing up on end and that people would notice this and wonder about it. He became so anxious and uncomfortable that he rushed to the men's room to brush his hair flat with a wet comb, which allayed his discomfort so that he could go back to his place. But soon the feeling that his hair was standing up returned and he had to make another attempt to brush it down. The symptom became so tortuous that he finally avoided going to public places where he had to remove his hat. This symptom and the impotence made him seek help at the psychoanalytic ambulatorium, where Dr. Hitschmann assigned him to me for analysis. I started his treatment in December 1925.

The patient was very cooperative and quickly developed a positive transference. When I made the first interpretation, I was delighted by its immediate, almost magical effect. I suggested to the patient that the erection that was missed in his penis was displaced to his hair, whereupon this symptom disappeared. The patient was greatly relieved and responded to this "miracle cure" with a very intense, erotically tinged transference love and admiration. However, he remained impotent. The material that he produced consisted of a repetitive declaration of his affection and loving admiration for the analyst, so the therapeutic process came to a standstill. I felt that the patient used this exaggerated positive transference to resist the exploration of deeper unconscious layers of his mind, but I did not know how to deal with his transference resistance. I therefore reported the case material in Wilhelm Reich's technical seminar.

Reich pointed out that in the material that I presented there was a mockingly hostile, contemptuous attitude toward the analyst that was covered up by the loud manifestations of love transference. Reich's unusual acuity in sensing hidden or disguised hostility and his didactic skill made me aware of the indications of the patient's hostility toward me. When my "third ear" was thus attuned to the manifestations of the patient's underlying hostility, I began to interpret signs of it to the patient. This made him very anxious, and he intensified his manifestations of positive feelings for me until one interpretation had a shocking effect on him. In one of the sessions he related that he used only the L or M streetcar line to come to treatment, although there was a series of other lines leading over the same route. He explained that *l* and *m* were significant because they are the first letters of the words *liebe mich* (love me), expressing the need for being loved by the analyst. I then pointed out that the most common expression of contempt in German also starts with *l* and *m*, namely *Leck mich*, an abbreviated form *of Leck mich am Arsch,* which corresponds to the English "kiss my ass." The patient reacted to this in a most dramatic way. After a few seconds of silence while he put his thumb in his vest pocket, he suddenly screamed and jerked his thumb out of his vest, and blood was running down his hand. He explained that a few days ago he had put a wrapped razor blade in his pocket to use at his place of employment. He had forgotten about it when he put his thumb into his pocket. When I pointed out the negative significance of *l* and *m*, he unconsciously used the "forgotten" razor blade for a bloody demonstration of the danger of castration to which my effort to uncover his hostile attitude toward me exposed him. I had to bandage his finger and send him to a medical emergency station, where the attendants took several stitches.

Such dramatic events are not often observed in analyses. This one impressed itself deeply on my young analytic mind. During many months following this incident, the patient expressed his hostility against the analyst, first timidly and haltingly, later in the form of open invective and accusation. It was possible to make the patient recognize his hostility as transferred to the analyst from his harsh and punitive father. After a few years of treatment, the patient was restored to mental health; he married his girlfriend, and they had two children when I left Vienna in 1938. He and his family, like so many of my Jewish patients, perished in the Holocaust.

My first report on this case in the technical seminar must have given the impression that I had the potential of becoming a psychoanalyst under proper guidance, for after the seminar Helene Deutsch told me that she would like to supervise a case of mine. I readily agreed to this. Wilhelm Reich also offered to supervise the case that I had presented. Both offered to work with me gratuitously, as they were aware that my hospital salary would not enable me to pay for supervision. Thus, I obtained supervision by two of the leading analysts in Vienna.

I took a third case, which I reported to Helene Deutsch, who was then director of the institute. I had had about ten hours of supervision with her when she told me that she was going on a trip to Italy and would have to interrupt the supervision and that it was time for me to find my therapeutic orientation with the patient unaided. I remember her saying, "If you have not learned it by now, you will never learn it," or words to that effect. The supervision of my second case continued in Reich's seminar. Altogether I had approximately twenty-five individual supervision hours. This is in great contrast to the training in modern institutes, where two hundred to three hundred supervision hours are obligatory.

I attended the technical seminar for twelve more years and reported on several cases. I consider the continuous case seminar the most essential part of psychoanalytic training if it is conducted by an analyst with vast experience and supervisory talent. The seminar provides insight into the material and therapeutic guidance for the reporting student; it also lets all of the attending students participate in the analysis of a patient in addition to the analyses that they conduct themselves under supervision.

The case that I first presented in Reich's seminar and that later was supervised by him became the basis for a formal paper on latent negative transference, which I presented at the last session of Reich's technical seminar of the summer semester in 1926. It was well received; Anna Freud, who sat beside me when I presented it, said during the applause: *"Ausgezeichnet"* (excellent). I do not know whether this remark was addressed to me or was just a self-directed exclamation. However, I heard it and it made me feel very good. (The paper was published in *Internationale Zeitschrift fur Psychoanalyse* 13 [1927], under the title "Ueber latente, negative Uebertragung" [On latent negative transference]. It has never been translated into English.)

As a consequence of my presentation of this paper, Wilhelm Reich asked me whether I was willing to leave the hospital where I still worked as a resident and take on a similar position at the psychoanalytic ambulatorium. It was the first time that the financial situation of the ambulatorium, which had been functioning on a referral basis, allowed for the establishment of salaried positions. The salary would be somewhat less than what I received at the hospital, but Reich indicated that additional private patients would gradually increase my income considerably. My obligation would consist of conducting five analyses of patients who had applied for treatment at the ambulatorium. In addition, I would function as outpatient consultant twice a week for two evening hours at the Herzstation. Mine was one of three appointments (the others were Grete Bibring and Eduard Kronold) that established the first professional staff of the analytic clinic in Vienna. I accepted the offer without hesitation, since it gave me the opportunity to devote myself fully to the work of my vocational choice.

The medical examination rooms of the heart clinic served in the afternoon as offices for the analytic patients treated by the staff members of the psychoanalytic ambulatorium. There were no couches in the rooms and the analysand had to use a movable step to climb up to the examination table. There were no springs in the thin mattress on the table top. But the analysand was not the only one who had to endure the hardness of the makeshift arrangement for treatment: the analyst had to sit on a simple wooden chair without armrests, and after five sessions he felt the effects of so long a contact with the hard surface. In these surroundings, we demonstrated that the result of analytic work does not depend on the physical ambience; my colleagues and I conducted many successful analyses under these primitive conditions. Even older and experienced members of the analytic group worked under circumstances that would hardly be found acceptable nowadays. I remember that we once held the Kinderseminar at the apartment of Hermann Nunberg, who was then already a well-known figure in our science. Nunberg complained that bedbugs had established themselves in his bed, which during the day served as his analytic couch, and that he would have to do something about it. (Bedbugs were quite common in older Viennese houses.)

When I left the residency at the hospital and joined the staff of the ambulatorium, I had the mornings free and could use them to get more psychiatric experience. With the permission of Wagner von Jauregg, the head of psychiatry at the university hospital, I joined the rounds conducted by Paul Schilder. Schilder was full of brilliant ideas and his scholarship was of an incredible productivity. He distributed the reprints of his papers so frequently that we asked each other jokingly: "Have you already seen today's Schilder?" His creativity was so abundant that it was said that once, when there was only standing room in a streetcar, he wrote standing up while the car moved and had to be ordered by the conductor to stop his writing because his open fountain pen might endanger other passengers. Schilder's ideas were always original. His frequent remarks about other persons, particularly professional colleagues, were sharp and full of irony. However, what impressed me most and made the contact with him so valuable was the astuteness of his clinical observations and the wealth of his psychiatric knowledge. From the rounds with him I gained a great deal of psychiatric and psychodynamic understanding. I remember particularly his observation concerning the aggressive energy that is necessary for creative thinking, because creativity consists of breaking up old patterns and configurations and composing a new gestalt from the fragments.

Many of the younger psychiatrists on the staff of Wagner von Jauregg's clinic had become psychoanalysts or underwent psychoanalytic training. Among these were Heinz Hartmann, Edward Bibring, Otto Isakower, and later Erwin Stengel. Princess Marie Bonaparte joined Schilder's rounds during a certain period. The older associate and assistant professors of the department must have felt uncomfortable being surrounded by followers of Freud and they tried to defend themselves by outspoken hostility toward analysis. They attacked psychoanalysis wherever they saw an opportunity. But the importance of the application of psychoanalytic principles in psychiatry grew despite their resistive effort. Modern psychiatry, inasmuch as it is still psychologically oriented, is based on Freud's fundamental findings.

I took the job at the psychoanalytic ambulatorium in September 1926, and I was married in December. At that time, Editha was in psychoanalytic training at the institute. Her special interest was the therapy of children, for which she was particularly gifted. She discussed her cases regularly with Anna Freud. Soon Marianne Rie-Kris joined these sessions, which became a regular part of the curriculum of the institute. Annie Angel-

42

Katan, Jenny Pollack-Waelder, Edith Buxbaum, and Dorothy Tiffany-Burlingham also joined these seminars which took the official title "Seminar for Child Analysis."

In addition to her official training, Editha accompanied Vorstand (director) August Aichhorn when he worked as a child guidance counselor in educational institutions in Vienna. Soon Aichhorn entrusted her with conducting child guidance consultations on her own. One of the professors at the gymnasium where she counseled students, Fritz Redl, became interested in the analytic approach and went into training analysis with me. He has since gained world renown for his work in the psychopathology of delinquent groups.

Editha also held a salaried job as editor and proofreader at the Internationale Psychoanalytischer Verlag (publishing house). With our combined salaries, we were able to establish ourselves as a married couple. We could afford to rent an apartment in the sixth district of Vienna, where I had lived since birth. For the first time in my life I had a telephone and a decent bathroom and I felt *arrivé*. The analytic group cultivated social contact with one another and Editha and I welcomed the opportunity to participate in a social life where we both felt warmly received. The interests of most of our colleagues, like our own, widely transcended our professional area. In the analytic group we were associated with highly educated people. We could share our interests in art, literature, and music with them.

By June of 1925, I had become an associate member of the Psychoanalytic Society, although I was only at the beginning of my training at the institute. Two years later, I graduated from the institute and received a certificate signed by Helene Deutsch as the director. The document was also signed by Sigmund Freud in his function as president of the Vienna Psychoanalytic Society. His longhand script reads: "Fuer die Wiener Psychoanalytische Vereinigung—Prof. Freud, Obmann" (for the Vienna Psychoanalytic Society—Prof. Freud, President). Dr. Grete Bibring and I were the first trainees to graduate from the institute and we remained the only ones whose diplomas were signed by Freud himself. Similar institutes in other countries objected to the fact that the Vienna graduates alone had their diplomas signed by Freud, whereupon he stopped signing the certificates.

From early puberty on I had been an enthusiastic admirer of Gothic art. Austria had plenty of Gothic churches filled with precious sculptures and paintings of the fourteenth and fifteenth centuries. Although I was never a religious believer, I had always felt deeply moved by the spirituality expressed in these creations of the last period of the medieval epoch. When I began to read psychoanalytic literature, the application of psychoanalysis to works of art had a particular attraction for me. Sigmund Freud's "Leonardo da Vinci" and his analysis of the Moses statue of Michelangelo as well as Otto Rank's brochure "Der Kuenstler" (the artist) and Karl Abraham's work on Segantini, had made a deep impression on me and had motivated me to try to apply my scant knowledge of analysis to the creations of my favorite period of art. At that time I had only superficial knowledge of both psychoanalysis and art history of the middle ages. The result was the paper "Zur Analyse der Gotik" (Analysis of Gothic art). It was in every sense a dilettantish undertaking.

Editha recommended that I show the paper to Dr. Otto Rank, which I did. Unfortunately, Rank found it interesting enough to publish in *Imago* (1925). It appeared as the first paper of a special issue devoted to applications of psychoanalysis to representative art. In this way I was introduced as a psychoanalytic author of sorts before I was analyzed and when I was very poorly educated in both Gothic art and psychoanalysis. A few years later, Ernst Kris, then still curator at the Kunsthistorische Museum in Vienna, took it upon himself to show me the methodological impossibilities in the paper and made it very clear to me how inappropriate and dilettantish was my approach to such a gigantic field of human creativity as the Gothic period.

I let pass quite some time of growth and maturation during my analysis before I wrote my second paper. This effort was a report on a repetitive examination dream—my own—whose dynamic sources were different from the ones that Freud mentions in his *Interpretation of Dreams:* my examination dreams were not dreams of consolation. In his *Interpretation of Dreams,* Freud mentions the examination dream among the typical dreams.[*] In this type of dream one has to take an examination,

---

[*]*Standard Edition,* vol. 4, pp. 273-76

most often in one of the subjects of the *Matura*. Freud agrees with Wilhelm Stekels's observation that in this dream, which is experienced with anxiety and feelings of inadequacy, the subject is regularly one that the dreamer has passed successfully. The dream occurs the night before the dreamer has to fulfill an important, often crucial, life task. According to Freud, the dream expresses consolation and reassurance by pointing out that an earlier task that had been dreaded had been accomplished successfully.

My dreams were about the *Matura*, which I had dreaded as a final reckoning. I had been a rather poor student in the gymnasium. It was the only way I could dare to express my resentment of my father, who was professor at a lyceum, an institution of learning that corresponded to the gymnasium. He expected my brother and me to be honor students, as he himself had been. I dreaded the *Matura*, where I would certainly be flunked because of my many lacunae of knowledge in the different subjects. It loomed over all the years in the gymnasium as a day of reckoning, a *dies irae, dies illa*.

I was drafted into the army shortly before the *Matura* and obtained the graduation certificate without having to take the examination. I thus escaped the final showdown and punishment. Instead, the dream, with all its anguish, occurred repeatedly through the years until my analysis cured me of this nightly torture. My analyst suggested that I write a paper about this examination dream, which, though its manifest aspect is typical of this type of dream, was dreamed by someone who never took the examination that he failed in his dream. My paper appeared in an issue of *Internationale Zeitschrift fuer Psychoanalyse* under the title "Ein Pruefungstraum" ("an examination dream").[*]

From 1924 to 1925, the Psychoanalytic Publishing House was preparing an edition of all of Freud's psychoanalytic works, to be published on the occasion of Freud's seventieth birthday, 6 May 1926. It was a luxurious undertaking that filled ten volumes. The work was titled *Gesammelte Schriften von Sigmund Freud*. Each volume was organized according to subject, not chronologically. A. J. Storfer, the director of the publishing house, was a genial man full of brilliant ideas and endowed with an indefatigable

---

[*]*Internationale Zeitschrift fuer Psychoanalyse* 13 (1927).

working capacity. The *Gesammelte Schriften* was the culmination of his work as a publisher. It was very carefully edited and printed in easily readable type. It was a unique event that a great scientific pioneer could see his revolutionary life work printed in its totality in such a beautiful form. Among us analysts, the edition was commonly called the *Gesamtausgabe* (complete edition).

Storfer had planned that the eleventh volume of the *Gesamtausgabe* would be an index of all Freud's psychoanalytic papers. For this purpose, single volumes were given to different analysts for indexing. Although I was not yet a member of the society, Storfer gave me a share of the indexing task: volume 7, containing the "Introductory Lectures"; volume 4, containing the "Psychopathology of Everyday Life" and "On the History of the Psychoanalytic Movement"; and two smaller publications, "On Psychoanalysis" (the five lectures Freud gave in 1909 at Clark University, in Worcester, Massachusetts), and "The Interest in Psychoanalysis." The very careful reading that the task demanded gave me a detailed knowledge of Freud's writings. To index the two volumes, I had to read Freud with thoroughness and careful consideration of every sentence. This gave me the opportunity to recognize the depth of the content and to enjoy the beauty of Freud's style. From then on, I continued to read other works of Freud with equal care, and as a psychoanalytic teacher I always tried to instruct my students to read with the same thoroughness. The result of such a careful reading of Freud's works for the psychoanalyst is invaluable.

After Storfer received the indexes of the ten volumes of the *Gesamtausgabe* it was necessary to combine them for the planned last volume, containing the final index. He farmed out the different letters of the alphabet to different analysts for compilation. The letters S and T fell to Editha and me. It was a laborious task, much less interesting and profitable than the indexing of the single volumes. Editha and I did the work during our summer vacation in 1926. We were modestly remunerated, but every increase of our income was welcome.

The edition of the ten volumes was very expensive, and it was printed in a very limited edition. Storfer's grandiose projects created an additional burden for the financial situation of the publishing house. The operation drifted more and more into the red, although Freud had never taken any royalties for his written works since the foundation of the publishing house, so all of the receipts went back into the business. In the early thirties, Storfer was finally asked to resign. He was replaced by Freud's son Martin as the director. In one of our meetings Freud spoke with real regret about Storfer's leaving the Verlag. He said: "We feel like subjects of a 'Duodez-Fuersten,' after they have chased out their princely ruler." (Until 1870, Germany consisted of a series of loosely connected sovereign states, each ruled by a king or duke or prince. There were so many that jokingly one called the rulers, particularly of the small principalities, *"Duodez-Fuersten"*— dozen princes.) Freud continued: "Only after their prince is driven out do the former subjects realize how much they owe him. Here he had established a museum, there a beautiful library or magnificent castles." And the *Gesamtausgabe* certainly was a princely, beautiful work created during the time when Storfer headed the *Verlag.*

Since Freud continued writing after his seventieth birthday, one more volume had to be published in 1934, so the *Gesamtausgabe* finally numbered twelve volumes. In 1935, a new volume was printed and the index had to be supplemented for every new volume. The index should have appeared as volume 14. However, the Anschluss interrupted the work on the index, and it was never taken up again. Only part of it had been printed; the rest existed only in manuscript. Storfer gave me a partly printed, partly typed copy of the final index as a compensation when he abandoned his partnership with me on the psychoanalytic dictionary. I don't know if another copy exists.

Richard Sterba in 1927, the year he became a member of the Vienna Psychoanalytic Society. (Photo Lena Schur.)

Editha Sterba, 1927. (Photo Lena Schur.)

Richard Sterba as a medical student, 1919.

Coffee outside at the Innsbruck Psychoanalytic Congress, 1927. Members of the Vienna Psychoanalytic Society are seated with analysts from Berlin, Hungary, and Switzerland. The Viennese analysts are identified as follows: (*seated along right of table*) Grete Bibring, unknown, Jenny Pollack-Waelder, two unknown persons, (*with hat*) Helene Deutsch; (*along left of table facing away*) Editha Sterba, (*standing*) Wilhelm Reich, two unknown persons, (*with tight-fitting cap*) the first Mrs. Fenichel, Otto Isakower, Annie Angel-Katan, Otto Fenichel, (*standing in rear*) Richard Sterba.

Swimming at a lake in Carinthia Province in Austria, August 1928. (*Left to right*) maid, Wilhelm Reich, Eva Reich, Editha Sterba, Annie Reich, Richard Sterba.

On a Danube beach at Gaensehaeufel, September 1928, (*Left to right*) Dr. Tuchfeld (a trainee of the institute), Mrs. Tuchfeld, (*standing*) Annie Reich, (*standing, throwing ball*) Wilhelm Reich, (*seated, facing left*) Annie Angel-Katan, Edith Buxbaum, Editha Sterba, Eva Reich, Richard Sterba.

54

Aggstein (ruins) on the Danube, March 1930. Annie Reich and Richard
Sterba.

Train station at Davos, in the Swiss Alps, 1931. (*Left to right*) Annie Reich, Wilhelm Reich, Richard Sterba, Steffi [?, later Eduard Kronold's wife], Editha Sterba.

56

Liesl Kraus (sister-in-law of Max Schur), Wilhelm Reich, Annie Reich, Richard Sterba, Steffi [?, later Eduard Kronold's wife], Editha Sterba, Eduard Kronold.

In front of the Votiv-Kirche, Vienna, February 1929. (*Left to right*) Alfred Winterstein, Robert Waelder, Eduard Hitschmann, Richard Sterba, Hans Jokl, Edmund Bergler, A. J. Storfer.

Skiing trip at Davos, 1931. (*Left to right*) Liesl Kraus, Eduard Kronold, Editha Sterba, Annie Reich, Steffi [?, later Eduard Kronold's wife].

Docent Dr. Sigm. Freud

beehrt sich anzuzeigen, dass er von Mitte
September 1891 an

IX. Berggasse 19,

wohnen und daselbst von 5 – 7 Uhr (auch
8 – 9 Uhr Früh) ordiniren wird.

WIEN, Datum des Poststempels.

"Docent Dr. Sigm. Freud has the honor to announce that, from the middle of September 1891, he will live at 9 Berggasse 19, and will have office hours there from 5 to 7 P.M. (also 8-9 A.M.), Vienna, date of postmark."

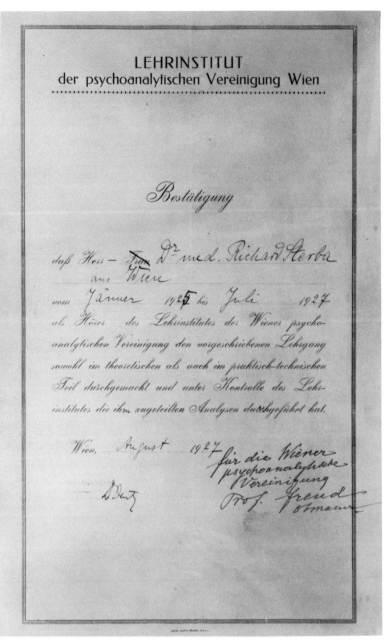

Richard Sterba's certificate of graduation in 1927, signed by Sigmund
Freud and Helene Deutsch.

At the Federns in Goisern, 1928. (*Left to right*) unknown, Mrs. Federn, Editha Sterba, Richard Sterba, Edward Bibring, Grete Bibring, Lehner [?, Grete Bibring's brother].

Freud signed this portrait (with ink spot) for Sterba in 1936.

mutter keine Frucht enthält, in ihrer Größe kaum zugenommen hat, daß keine kindlichen Herztöne und objektiv keine Kindesbewegungen wahrnehmbar sind. Die Aufklärung über das Nichtvorhandensein einer Schwangerschaft bringt die Phänomene der eingebildeten Schwangerschaft meist rasch zum Schwinden. Ein starker Wunsch nach dem Kind, der auch unbewußt sein kann, ist die wichtigste Grundlage für das Zustandekommen der eingebildeten Schwangerschaft, die der Konversionshysterie (s. d.) zuzurechnen ist.

Größenwahn (megalomania, delusions of grandeur; délire des grandeurs, mégalomania)

Der Größenwahn ist entsprechend dem Verlust der Realitätsprüfung, der ihm zugrunde liegt, ein psychotisches Symptom. Wahnhafte Größenideen finden sich vor allem bei Paranoia und Schizophrenie, auch bei organischen Psychosen, so etwa bei progressiver Paralyse. Die Größenideen sind der Ausdruck einer pathologischen Überschätzung des Ichs. Je nach dem Grade dieser Überschätzung sind sie verschieden intensiv, von der einfachen Überzeugung, an Leistung, Schönheit, Fähigkeiten, anderen weit über das Tatsächliche hinaus überlegen zu sein, bis zu phantastischen Vorstellungen, Gott zu sein, Milliarden zu besitzen, der Welterlöser zu sein u. dgl. m.

Die Selbstüberschätzung, aus der der Größenwahn folgt, hat eine Parallele in der Sexualüberschätzung, die im Zustande der Verliebtheit das geliebte Objekt über alle anderen erhebt und als das einzig Wertvolle erscheinen läßt, indem sie unser Urteil durch die positiven Affekte, die wir dem geliebten Objekt zuwenden, zu seinen Gunsten trübt und uns für seine Mängel und Fehler blind macht. Aus der libidinösen Grundlage der Überschätzung des Objekts in der Verliebtheit ist zu schließen, daß auch die Selbstüberschätzung, die dem Größenwahn zugrundeliegt, libidinöse Ursachen haben muß. Psychoanalytische Untersuchungen ergaben, daß die wesentlichen Veränderungen im Libidohaushalt bei jenen Psychosen, bei denen typischerweise Größenwahn auftritt, darin bestehen, daß die Libido von den Objekten abgezogen und dem Ich zugewendet wird. Diese abnorme Steigerung der narzißtischen Besetzung des Ichs ist die libidinöse Grundlage für die pathologische Selbstüberschätzung, der der Größenwahn entspricht; sie bildet das narzißtische Gegenstück zur Verliebtheit. Da die pathologische narzißtische Ichbesetzung der Psychosen eine Regression auf den Zustand des kindlichen Narzißmus darstellt, muß man erwarten, daß hohe Selbsteinschätzung und Größenwahn auch beim Kind gefunden werden. Dies ist in der Tat der Fall.

Das magische Denken des Kindes (s. Magie), sein Glauben an die Allmacht der Gedanken (s. d.) und an die Zauberkraft der Worte sind der Ausdruck der Selbstüberschätzung vermöge der hohen libidinösen Besetzung des kindlichen Ichs. Beim Primitiven, der psychologisch der kindlichen Stufe der Menschheitsentwicklung entspricht, finden wir dieselbe hohe, libidinöse Besetzung des Ichs und dementsprechend Größenideen

Sample dictionary entry from *Handwörterbuch der Psychoanalyse*, no. 5 (Vienna: Internationaler Psychoanalytischer Verlag, 1936), entry "Megalomania."

Reproduction of Freud's introduction to the *Handwörterbuch*.

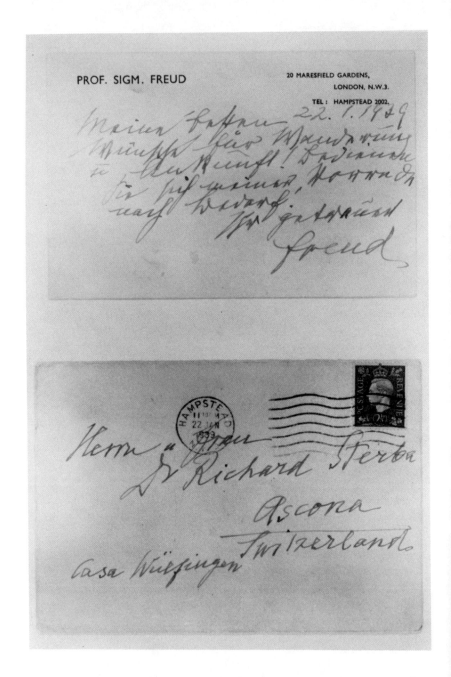

Card and envelope from Freud to Sterba, 21 January 1939, giving Sterba permission to use Freud's introduction in the *Handwörterbuch*.

III. Vienna Psychoanalytic Society Meetings

THE EFFECTS OF FREUD'S SHIFTS IN THINKING ON THE NEW SCIENCE

Until the early 1930s, the official meetings of the Psychoanalytic Society took place every second Wednesday in the lecture room of the Herzstation. When I started to attend the meetings in the fall of 1924, relatively early in my analysis, the membership was still small and could easily be seated in the lecture room. But the number grew rapidly, particularly after 1926 when the institute was well established, and more and more chairs had to be brought in, so the room became very crowded. Finally, the clinic administration objected to our presence there, at least as far as the meetings were concerned. A more adequate room for the society meetings was found in the medical district a few blocks away, but we continued to occupy the Herzstation for the functions of the ambulatorium and institute.

The meetings themselves fell into three categories: presentation of original papers, discussion of Freud's recent publications, and presentation of brief communications.

ORIGINAL PAPERS

Original papers were presented by the members of the society or guest speakers. When one looks through the reports of the meetings of the Vienna Psychoanalytic Society in the yearly volumes of *Internationale Zeitschrift* or *International Journal of Psychoanalysis*, it is amazing to see the number of original contributions by the members in the twenties and thirties. I will mention only a few of the papers that impressed me particularly, in the order in which they occur to me. Occasionally I will make a short comment concerning my subjective reaction to them. To report their contents would fill another volume and would transcend the scope of the present undertaking.

One of the first papers I heard was presented by Helene Deutsch in 1924. It was called "The Psychology of Female Menopause." Several papers of hers following this one also dealt with female sexuality. They were the basis of much more extensive studies on the same subject. Helene Deutsch's paper on agoraphobia in 1928 presented new insight into this neurotic fear of open spaces. In another paper in 1929, "On the Genesis of Family Romance," she described an unusual form of this fantasy in which the fantasized parents are of a *lower* status than the real parents. Her paper "As-If Personalities" in the early 1930s first described and explained this character type not infrequently met in the clinical experience.

I remember Wilhelm Reich's paper "On the Impulse-Ridden Character," which he read in January 1925. Its excellent presentation of clinical material and psychodynamic explanation impressed me very much. In two papers in November 1925 and January 1926 he expounded his theory of the preventative and curative effects of a perfect orgasm. The papers, which were both called "The Psychic Disturbances of Orgasm," were to result in his book *The Function of Orgasm* (1927). In these papers he already showed his tendency to reduce the genesis of neurotic symptomology to a monocausal factor. In the discussions he more and more stubbornly refused to accept any argument that contradicted his theory. With his paper "The Genital-Narcissistic Character" in October 1926, Reich established this character type as a clinical concept. He read a paper on "The Overestimation of Trauma in Psychoanalysis" in February 1927.

In December 1926, Heinz Hartmann presented a paper titled "Some Methodological Questions of Psychoanalysis." His effort to introduce scientifically correct thinking in the new science was badly needed.

I gave a paper titled "Psychoanalytic Remarks concerning the Expression of Feeling for Nature by Goethe" in December

1927. I presented this paper in order to become a member of the society. I had noticed when I read Goethe's poems describing landscapes that the emotional effect of the beauty of his poems was particularly intense when the verses presented the objects acting in an anthropomorphic way. This was done so skillfully that the reader is hardly aware of the anthropomorphic presentation. The effect is an extension of the ego boundaries over the moving cosmic object, which provides a profoundly gratifying experience of the outside world. I called this esthetic mechanism "cosmic motility." The paper was favorably received and I became a member at the next business meeting.

In 1929 I read "The Dynamics of the Overcoming of Transference Resistance," which became the basis for the paper "The Fate of the Ego in Analytic Therapy," which I presented at the International Congress in Wiesbaden in 1932. In this paper I established the concepts of the "therapeutic ego split" and of the "therapeutic alliance," which became basic in the theory of psychoanalytic therapy.

I remember Robert Waelder's papers "The Structural Viewpoint in Psychoanalysis" in May 1926 and "The Principle of Multiple Functioning: Observations on Overdetermination" in 1929, which have become essential parts of analytic theory. Waelder's methodological approach was a model of scientific thinking.

In November 1928, Edward Bibring read his paper "Clinical Contribution to the Problem of Paranoia: A Case of Organ Projection," which revealed his profound insight into the mode of functioning of the primary process in this psychosis.

Hermann Nunberg read his paper "The Synthetic Function of the Ego" in 1929, presenting a concept that has since been integrated into psychoanalytic thinking. I remember that in one of the scientific meetings, Freud spoke in connection with Nunberg's paper of a legend about a saint, Bishop Wolfgang. In this legend, the bishop orders the devil to carry the heavy stones from the field so that he can build a church, which later becomes a shrine. Freud compared himself with the devil, who did the heavy work, laboring to produce the building material, which we, his followers, then used for the structures of our theories.

Paul Schilder gave several papers in the late 1920s on the psychoanalytic explanation of psychotic phenomena. They seemed to me to have resulted from the series of lectures on psychoanalysis and psychosis which he gave to our first-year class at the Psychoanalytic Institute.

I was particularly impressed by a paper on the "Psychology of Pity" in which Ludwig Jekels, in January 1930, made a splendid synthesis of the contradictory evaluations of this phenomenon by various philosophers. I remember Eduard Hitschmann's "On the Psychology of Jewish Jokes" in May 1930, and Siegfried Bernfeld's "On Psychophysiological Research" in November 1932.

Paul Federn gave several reports on his observations of ego feelings and ego boundaries. On 2 December 1931, he read the paper "Ego Feelings in the Dream;" in September 1932 he read "The Ego Cathexis during Parapraxes," and in November 1933 "The Awakening of the Ego during Dreaming."

In November 1932, Ernst Kris presented a fascinating paper titled "A Psychotic Artist." It dealt with the eighteenth-century Austrian sculptor Franz Xaver Messerschmidt, who had become famous for his series of grimacing busts, which at the time were considered "physiognomic studies." They were in reality self-portraits expressing a psychotic defense against a passive fellatio delusion. In October 1934, Kris read his "Psychology of Biography," particularly of the great artists. I remember how impressed I was by his concept of the *gelebte vita*, the unconscious conducting of the life course of artists according to certain typical legends about great artists concerning the discovery of their talent and their further development.

In 1934, Felix Deutsch gave a paper, "On Euthanasia."

Three meetings in January and February of 1935 were devoted to a presentation by Anna Freud called "The Usefulness of Psychoanalytic Technique for the Study of the Mental Agencies."

In 1935, Otto Isakower reported on the typical sensations while falling asleep, known since then as the "Isakower phenomenon."

The report of the second analysis of the "Wolfman" by Ruth Mack-Brunswick was received with great interest. However, I personally was disappointed, because I could not help comparing Mack-Brunswick's report with Freud's "History of an Infantile Neurosis." Freud's was the most fascinating case history in all of psychoanalytic literature, and, as the German proverb says: "The better is the enemy of the good." However, I might not have been objective in my evaluation of Mack-Brunswick's reanalysis of the "Wolfman" because I had no particular fondness for her as a person, though I did not really know her well. Her ambitious sharpness, which I saw reflected in her facial expression, aroused a certain antagonism in me.

In 1937, Heinz Hartmann presented his paper "Ich-Psychologie und Anpassungsproblem" (Ego psychology and the problem of adaptation). It inaugurated the ego psychological approach, which would dominate the psychoanalytic scene in the forties and fifties.

Besides the presentations by members of the society, of which I have mentioned only a few, I remember some presentations by guest speakers. Sandor Ferenczi came from Budapest and reported on his newest therapeutic approach based on his theory that a lack of adequate love in the parental care of a child is the deepest cause of any neurosis. In therapy Ferenczi tried to undo the damage of infantile love privation by giving the patient as much parental love as possible. Ferenczi reported a scene from the analysis of an adult male who, in a trancelike state, put his arm around Ferenczi and asked him: "Grandpa, can boys have babies?" Ferenczi answered with most moving kindness: "My child, why do you think so?" One has to have known the lovable personality of Ferenczi to recognize how much fatherly affection was expressed in this reply. When in the discussion somebody remarked that, considering the infantile insatiability for affection in such a regressed state, one could have only a single patient, Ferenczi gave the amazing answer: "Yes, one should really have only one patient." This statement surprised us all; however, as far as I remember, nobody contradicted it, because we knew that Ferenczi was not a well person at that time (he suffered from pernicious anemia). It seemed to me that Ferenczi's great merits as a pioneer, a brilliant observer, and a bold entrepreneur in creative psychoanalytic thinking silenced the objections to his gross deviation from Freud's classical therapeutic approach. We all had the feeling that our cause had lost this great creative mind. Freud, in his eulogy of Ferenczi in 1933, says about the last period of

Ferenczi's therapeutic endeavors, "Our friend drifted away from us." How deeply this deviation of his friend and collaborator must have grieved Freud.

A very charming episode occurred in the late twenties after a society meeting in which Ferenczi had presented a paper. A group of us went with Ferenczi to a nightclub at which the famous American dancer Josephine Baker was performing. We all enjoyed the graceful, supple movement of her beautiful body and were enthusiastic about her performance. After her appearance on the stage, Josephine Baker joined the audience. I have no idea what made her pick out Ferenczi for an enchanting little scene. She came to our table and in a most natural fashion sat on Ferenczi's lap. She glided her hand through her own black hair, which was smoothly and tightly glued to her scalp by a heavy pomade. Then she stroked the bald center of Ferenczi's head and, rubbing the pomade on his hairless scalp, said, "So, that will make your hair grow." Ferenczi and our whole group thoroughly enjoyed this episode; Josephine Baker's irresistible charm made inoffensively humorous what otherwise could have been considered an impudent transgression.

Joan Rivière from London presented to our society a paper on the theories and technique of Melanie Klein. Klein's ideas were not found acceptable by the Viennese group, although a serious attempt was made by the Viennese analysts to reconcile her approach with our classical analysis. In fact, Robert Waelder once traveled to London to represent to the British Society of Psychoanalysis the objections of the Viennese group to Klein's approach. The parties could not agree on basic issues and the two camps are still incompatible. However, some of Klein's tenets on the very early phases of the mother-child relationship are in harmony with the object-relation theory that has been developed recently. Perhaps the future will bring more of a rapprochement. However, I cannot imagine that the assumption of complicated concept formations in the first few months of life will be found acceptable by classical analysts.

Otto Fenichel came as a guest from Berlin and presented a paper rich in clinical material and instructive in its technical content. Another of the guest speakers was Hans Kelsen, the great scholar of constitutional law. He was a professor at the law school

of the Vienna University and was one of the authors of the consti-
tution of the Austrian Republic. He spoke to our society on "The
Concept of the State and Psychoanalysis." One sentence from his
interesting paper engraved itself deeply in my mind, because of its
precision, brevity, and ubiquitous validity: "Aus einem Sein-Satz
kann man keinen Soll-Satz ableiten" (freely translated, "from a
statement of facts one cannot deduce any moral guidelines").
When, many years later, I became acquainted with Kelsen in the
United States, I told him that his statement at the Vienna Society
meeting had made a lasting impression on me. He replied: "I can
only wish that more people would remember this axiom and heed
it." Once in our conversations I remarked that I did not have a
scientific head, for I just cannot sit in libraries and look up references for hours on end. To this he replied: "It is not a scientific
mind that is missing in you. You have no scientific behind."

Marie Bonaparte, Princess of Greece and Denmark, presented in November 1927 a paper on the "Symbolism of Head
Trophies," with fascinating examples ranging from the rituals of
the most primitive savages to the hunting costume and strict rituals performed by hunters in the Western world, where the hunt
was a sport of the aristocracy and the upper classes. I was particularly impressed by the ingenious interpretation of the expression
Jemandem die Hoerner aufsetzen (putting antlers of a stag on
somebody, referring to a husband who is being cuckolded). The
stag is considered the king of the hunting grounds, and the collo-
quial expression turns the cuckolded man into a father representative and thus gives the cuckolding Oedipal significance.

DISCUSSION OF FREUD'S
RECENT PUBLICATIONS

The second category of the society meetings consisted of
reports on and discussions of Freud's most recent publications.
They often surpassed in importance the meetings in which original papers were presented. The period of which I am speaking is
one of the most revolutionary in Freud's own scientific development. Most remarkable was the radical change brought about by

the recognition of aggression as a drive in its own right. It always amazes me how, late in his theoretical development, Freud acknowledged aggression as a drive equal to, if not of greater importance than, the libido. Freud said about himself in his writings that he had no inclination to cruelty and aggression, and that he even avoided scientific controversy. It is obvious that he was capable of sublimating a great part of his aggression, with which a scientific revolutionary of Freud's greatness must have been endowed. He obviously was transforming the aggressive drives into a strength of conviction and a firmness and perseverance in pursuing his goals and into maintaining the untiring and resourceful defense necessary to withstand the attacks on psychoanalysis from all different quarters.

Much of an analyst's aggressive drive can be absorbed in the work with his patients, although it must be sublimated and neutralized to "passionate patience"* and gentle but unrelenting insistence on bringing about an adaptive change in the patient's neurotic reaction patterns. However, in my opinion, there is an indication that Freud enjoyed aggression when expressed in literary form by others. He quoted with conspicuous frequency two German writers. One is Heinrich Heine, some of whose satirical, often nastily cynical remarks against authorities and contemporary writers Freud loved to quote, with noticeable delight. The second writer is Wilhelm Busch, also an excellent draftsman, who illustrated his own verses with very funny drawings. Freud enjoyed the slapstick descriptions and illustrations of mishaps that Busch's fictitious characters suffered either by accident or through two mischievous boys, "Max und Moritz," or by other malicious persons. The sadistic delight at the damage or injury inflicted on others by Busch's characters is so often referred to in Freud's books and papers that one cannot help assuming that Freud enjoyed them thoroughly. A strong inner defense against his own aggressive inclinations must have prevented him, I think, from recognizing the importance of aggression in human psychology earlier than 1921, that is, before *Beyond the Pleasure Principle* was published. This unwillingness to recognize the

---

*A term coined by Julius Huxley in his preface to *Living Free,* by Joy Adamson (New York: Harcourt Brace Jovanovich, 1961).

dynamic importance of the aggressive drive is particularly remarkable because many years earlier Alfred Adler had proclaimed aggression as an innate force in the human mind.

I would like to describe the impact that the works of Freud that appeared during the period under discussion had on our group of analysts. I hardly have to point out that some of the most important theoretical changes that occurred in the twenties and thirties required considerable adjustment of our analytic thinking. With *Beyond the Pleasure Principle*, Freud firmly established aggressive tendencies as the manifestations of a destructive drive on a par with the libido. However, for a number of years after its publication, analysts had great difficulty accepting this new orientation in the theory of drives. A particular difficulty arose from the fact that Freud linked the destructive urges to a biological concept, which he termed "death instinct." Up until then, analysts had learned to search in all psychopathological formations, as well as in neurotic behavior in general, for the libidinous drive strivings that were in conflict with self-preservative and moral tendencies. Freud's followers had been educated to become libido hunters and detectives. In his writings, Freud himself had emphasized this function of the analyst when he said, "The analyst has to follow the libido into its hideouts," and similar expressions for the analyst's task of discovering the culprit libido. When one reads the minutes of the society meetings taken by Otto Rank in the years 1908-1918 (recently translated and published by Hermann Nunberg and Ernst Federn), one is struck by the eagerness, ingenuity, and imagination with which the libido was hunted down in every mental manifestation.

In 1914, Freud, in his paper on narcissism, had extended the dynamic deployment of libidinous forces into the realm of the ego, which up until then was considered the agency that defended itself against the unacceptable libido manifestations. No wonder that some of the Viennese analysts had a hard time accepting the aggressive drive as an independent dynamic force. They continued to consider aggression a reaction to frustration, caused by external, mainly educational prohibitions and their incorporated continuation in the form of intrapsychic structures that opposed libidinous gratification "in loco parentis." Although Freud had said at the beginning of the last chapter of *Beyond the Pleasure*

Principle that the establishment of the concept of the death instinct was based on a far-reaching speculation, in later years he treated it more and more as part of his established theory.

Wilhelm Reich was the most vociferous defendant of the theory that aggression was caused solely by frustration. Some members of the Vienna group embraced the death instinct theory totally—for example, Paul Federn, who wanted to introduce the term *mortido* in analogy to the term *libido* for the hypothetical self-destructive *Ur*-drive. Hermann Nunberg was another proponent of the concept of the death instinct. The pro and con struggle concerning the establishment of the concept of the death instinct was still going on in the Viennese group when I entered the analytic scene. But just at that time a new theoretical shift in Freud's thinking had taken place with the publication of *The Ego and the Id* (1923). It confronted the analysts with a new task: the acceptance of an unconscious portion of the ego. Previously the ego had been considered congruent with the conscious and preconscious area of the mind. The new theoretical framework evolved with Freud's recognition that, while the source of all instinctual drives is unconscious, the repressive activity of the ego is also inaccessible to consciousness. The need to accept the new structural theory (which to a great extent replaced the topographical model that until then had been the foundation of Freud's metapsychology) met with great resistance. Some of the members refused to deal with it altogether. I remember that, in a theoretical discussion at a society meeting, Isidor Sadger, an older member, shouted indignantly: "I don't care a hoot whether the id represses the ego or the ego represses the id." He refused even to try to comprehend the change to new theoretical conceptions that Freud's *Ego and the Id* had forced upon us. For the younger generation, to which I belonged and which had not been working for many years with the systemic model of the psychic apparatus, it was easier to absorb the change to the structural theory. I found the new concept especially helpful for the understanding of resistances. The acknowledgment of an unconscious part of the ego makes it much easier to explain the effect of infantile, real, or imaginary dangers in the form of resistances of which the patient is not consciously aware.

Three years after the publication of *The Ego and the Id,*

Freud published another work that made a radical change in a fundamental part of our analytic thinking necessary: *Inhibition, Symptom, and Anxiety* (1926). It introduced a new theory of the origin of anxiety; in fact, it forced a complete turnabout of our theoretical thinking concerning the generation of anxiety. Up until then, the assumption was that the repression of drive energy resulted in the transformation of this energy into anxiety. In this way, the repression of libido was considered the cause of anxiety. This theory was derived from the ubiquitous observation that where a drive manifestation was to be expected, such as in a situation of temptation, anxiety often was experienced instead. From this observation, Freud had originally drawn the conclusion that as a result of the repression, the libido had been transformed into anxiety like wine into vinegar. In *Inhibition, Symptom, and Anxiety*, Freud turned around the repression-anxiety sequence: anxiety became the motivational cause of the repression of the drive. Thus, the *transformation* theory of anxiety was replaced by the *signal* theory. Neurotic anxiety is therefore a function of the ego generated as a warning of dangers that a certain drive gratification would bring about, a danger signal that motivates the ego to repress the dreaded drive. Neurotic anxiety is a signal of anticipated danger.

This theoretical reversal, the new structural model of mental anatomy, and the acknowledgment of aggression as a drive in its own right were three heavy impacts. They demanded fundamental changes in an analyst's theoretical thinking. These concepts profoundly increased our dynamic understanding while they brought about decisive changes in the therapeutic approach. In his work of 1926, Freud also restored the almost-abandoned term *defense* and made us more fully aware that other mechanisms besides repression, like isolation and undoing, had to be recognized as means frequently used to ward off dangerous instinctual strivings and prevent their gaining access to consciousness. With the new theory of anxiety, the power of the ego had to be gauged fundamentally different from Freud's evaluation of it in 1923, when in *The Ego and the Id* he had compared the ego with a poor rider who often has to pretend that he is guiding the horse where it actually wants to go by its own will. In contrast to this concept of relative helplessness, Freud in 1926 elevated the ego to a position of considerable control with the help of the powerful bridling effect of the anxiety signal, which mobilized the different forms of defense. The catch-phrase: "Wir werden von unserem Es gelebt" (we are lived by our id), which Georg Groddek had coined in his publication *Das Buch vom Es,* * before the publication of *The Ego and the Id,* had lost considerably its impressiveness and validity when Freud emphasized the mighty tool of the anxiety signal, which gives the ego power over inadmissable drive impulses of the id. The signal anxiety produced by the ego against dangerous id strivings was then the motor force for repression. The necessity to reverse the order *repression causes anxiety* to *anxiety motivates repression* was bewildering to some members of the group, since it necessitated the adaptation to a new way of theoretical understanding of clinical material. Wilhelm Reich, for instance, found the new theory of the dynamic relationship between repression and anxiety unacceptable.

The recognition of the power of aggression in mental activity deepened the insight into the dynamics of symptom formation. It added to the understanding of how the inner struggle between the antagonistic forces, libido and aggression, in their fusion and defusion leads to symptom formation. It helped us recognize how inner conflict contributes to character formation and expresses itself in group behavior, and how it generates creativity.

In 1927, Freud published his treatise on religion, *The Future of an Illusion,* which dealt with the irrationality of religious belief and the relationship of religion to civilization. He sent a copy of the little book to Oskar Pfister, a clergyman in Zurich, Switzerland, who was also a practicing psychoanalyst. In the copy Freud wrote a dedication: *"Zur Erbauung"* (for your edification). Pfister tried to argue against Freud's treatise with a paper titled "Die Illusion einer Zukunft" (The illusion of a future). In my opinion, the title was the best part of his paper; the content is hardly convincing. However, Freud's expectation of a future without the irrational, religious belief is not being realized. Even in

The Book of the Id: Psychoanalytic Letters to a Friend (Vienna: Internationaler Psychoanalytischer Verlag, 1923), published in English by Funk and Wagnalls, 1950.

enlightened people the need for the irrational, the magic, the illusionary seems to be stronger today than the need for reason and intellect, in whose power Freud believed so much.

In 1930, the publication of *Civilization and Its Discontents* had provided ample material for discussion in society meetings; so did *New Series of Introductory Lectures,* published in 1933. The reviews and discussions of these two works provided the content of a series of society meetings.

In addition to these major works, an amazing number of shorter works by Freud appeared during the years about which I am reporting. They are: "The Infantile Genital Organization: An Interpolation into the Theory of Sexuality" (1923), "Neurosis and Psychosis" (1924), "The Economic Problem of Masochism" (1924), "The Dissolution of the Oedipus Complex" (1924), "The Loss of Reality in Neurosis and Psychosis" (1924), "A Note upon the 'Mystic Writing-Pad' and Negation" (1925), "The Resistances of Psychoanalysis" (1925), "Some Psychological Consequences of the Anatomical Distinction between the Sexes" (1925), "An Autobiographical Study" (1925), "The Question of Lay Analysis" (1926), "Fetishism" (1927), "Humor" (1928), "A Religious Experience" (1928), "On Libidinous Types" and "On Female Sexuality" (1931), and "Constructions in Analysis" (1937). They were all published in *Internationale Zeitschrift fuer Psychoanalyse* and appeared in English in *International Journal of Psychoanalysis.*

One can well imagine that we analysts felt bombarded by the barrage of new ideas and the correction or enlargement of established ones to which Freud's productivity exposed us during this period. Even in some of the shorter papers of that time Freud opened up new vistas and new fields of exploration. An example is "On Female Sexuality," in which he acknowledged the fundamental importance for both sexes of the pre-Oedipal relationship to the mother. This paper, along with the work of others, laid the foundation for the object-relation studies that occupy so much analytic research.

The fecundity of Freud's creative genius during this period was amazing. Despite his cancer and the constant pain that he suffered, he kept analysts fully occupied with trying to understand and to absorb the new ideas he generated.

BRIEF COMMUNICATIONS

Interspersed between the society meetings devoted to the presentation of original papers and the discussions of Freud's recent publications was a third category of meetings in which brief communications were presented. They provided the opportunity for the members to present preliminary reports on original ideas or examples of clinical material and short papers on applied psychoanalysis concerning all kinds of human behavior. These meetings were always alive and stimulating: a wealth of creative thoughts, try-outs of new theoretical concepts, and clinical hypotheses alternated with reports on technical therapeutic subjects presented by the different members. Some communications were simply clinical subjects in the form of vignettes that illustrated, confirmed, or contradicted some recently established hypotheses. It was a very illustrious group of analytic minds that expressed themselves in a more informal and tentative way in these meetings. Here ideas were expressed in a seminal state where they would stimulate immediate response by others. The member could then test, enlarge, and organize them for later publication or a more formal presentation.

In general, the society meetings were peaceful and dignified. They were, after all, an assembly of *"gebildete"* people. The noun form of *gebildete, Bildung* is generally translated into English as "education." However, one would not call somebody who has merely graduated from the university a *gebildeter Mensch*. To be considered *gebildet,* one had to be able to speak at least two living languages (predominantly English and French) besides German, the language of the meetings; less important were Italian and Spanish. The knowledge of ancient Latin and Greek, the obligatory studies at the gymnasium, was taken for granted. A *gebildeter Mensch* had to be familiar with the most important works of Western literature and the most important events of the history of Western culture. He had to be familiar with its outstanding artists and their chefs d'oeuvre. Interest in and information about current events should not be missing. One expects a *Gebildeter* to be well mannered and to use the vocabulary of the *gebildete* circle. A great deal of the behavior, interests, and mentality of the *Gebildete* is absorbed from childhood on if he is brought up in a *gebildete* milieu; it is difficult to acquire it later. Of course, the *gebildete Mensch* as I have described him here was an ideal; however, most of the society members attained some degree of this *Bildung*. A few of them, like Bernfeld, Hartmann, Kris, and Waelder, even attained an unusual degree. Sigmund Freud was above all of us; his *Bildung* was of the highest level, as one can easily recognize in his publications and letters.

The *gebildete Mensch* as I have described him was the educational model of the liberal bourgeoisie in Austria—the background of most Viennese analysts. Most analysts were politically inactive although ideologically they were liberals. Their sympathies, like those of most Viennese intellectuals, were with the Social Democrats, who strove for an evolutionary socialization. The Social Democratic party held the majority in the city government of Vienna, where its social achievements were remarkable.

Freud's spirit and scientific seriousness hovered over us. His great personal dignity and respect-inspiring superiority, our common devotedness to the "cause," and the greatness of Freud's scientific edifice, of which we were constantly aware, obliged all of us to behave in a dignified manner. We were aware of being privileged to be near the creative source of the new science, which we knew was destined to have a decisive impact on our culture and was already a major factor in shaping modern Western thought and life in the twentieth century. The closeness to Freud's work *in statu nascendi* gave us the feeling of participation in a major, future-shaping scientific and cultural process. Each new publication by Freud renewed and intensified this emotion and, since the Viennese analysts all shared in it, the feeling of belonging to a community of privileged individuals was unavoidable. This led to a sense of unity and harmony among the members. Anna Freud's presence at the society meetings, which she chaired during her last years in Vienna, had a definite influence on the members. Her calm and collected demeanor, her superior intelligence, and her objective reserve became a model for practically all of us. In her presence, proper behavior was *de rigueur*—and not only because she was the great master's daughter. It was the genuine strength of her character and the moral force radiating from her that contributed to the atmosphere in the meetings. Her behavior was the result of her upbringing and development in Freud's highly cultured home and it set a certain standard for those of us who were sensitive to it.

Nevertheless, currents of antagonism between some members were noticeable, although they seldom broke out into the open. Wilhelm Reich's stubborn refusal to accept arguments contradicting his theories is a significant example. Particularly during the last two years before he left Vienna, Reich's sensitivity to contradiction and his readiness to react to scientific counterarguments as if they were personal attacks sometimes disturbed the scientific calm of the meetings. On such occasions he became extremely pale and his facial expression betrayed that he was hardly able to control his rage.

Theodor Reik occasionally played the *enfant terrible* when he expressed open hostility toward his medical colleagues. He had "only" a nonmedical university degree. As some lay analysts easily do, he developed an open animosity toward physician analysts. From what I could observe, his feeling of being treated as a second-rate citizen by his M.D. analytical colleagues was unjustified, although his arrogant and derisive attitude in the society provoked antagonism among the other members. Even Freud, who had very high regard for Reik's ability and achievement, once wrote him the following letter, which Reik himself published in *The Search Within* (New York: Farrar, Straus & Cudahy, 1956). Reik wrote: "I had written a letter full of bitterness against some colleagues who had hurt my pride, and I had given uninhibited expression to my indignation. Freud's letter was, of course, well justified in its criticism of my attitude." Then Reik quotes Freud's letter:

Tegel, September 13, 1982

Dear Herr Doctor:
   I cannot explain your attitude except in the following way. You send me those remarks, submit yourself to my decision as to whether they should be printed, and anticipate that I shall condemn them as unworthy of you in form and content. In doing that you give expression to your feelings and discharge them without any risk.
   The calculation is correct, but it grieves me much that you even need such therapy. Your hostility transgresses all justified measure, blasts the frontiers of what is permissible,

spoils your presentation, and must sadden anyone who, as I, has the interest of a friend in you and highly appreciates your achievements. It cannot possibly go on like that.

I would have asked you long ago to see me, but I am at present in a bad state of transition, still unable to do anything and compelled to hide like a crab that changes its shell.

Cordially yours,
Freud

I quote Freud's letter here because it characterizes Reik's provocative attitude. It is interesting that Reik himself published Freud's letter and found it justified. However, I do not think it changed his attitude and behavior, which were notoriously arrogant. I hear that when he went into exile from the Nazis and settled in Holland, he caused a split in the psychoanalytic community during his stay there. After he left Holland for the United States, the Dutch analytic community was unified again. Because of Reik's arrogant and provocative behavior, he was not accepted as a member of the American Psychoanalytic Association, whereas other European lay analysts (like Siegfried Bernfeld, Robert Waelder, Ernst Kris, Erik Erikson, Edith Buxbaum, and Editha Sterba) had no difficulty becoming members. Reik then founded a society of his own. He was a brilliant analytic thinker but unbridled in his contempt of his colleagues, particularly of the medical doctors.

Between Paul Federn and Helene Deutsch there existed an enmity that was from time to time expressed in remarks they made about each other to other members. Helene Deutsch was such an outstanding personality and central figure that I cannot forego talking about her more in my tales about the Vienna psychoanalytic group. In Chapter IV I will speak about her almost uncanny ability to recognize and predict unconscious contents and dynamic currents. I cannot avoid mentioning here some other features of which I became aware in my experiences with her.

Helene Deutsch sometimes made mocking and ridiculing remarks about persons whom she disliked, and she did it with visible delight in her witty invectives. I was unpleasantly surprised when I first heard one of her remarks about Paul Federn. Federn, on the other hand, made hostile remarks about Helene Deutsch that were neither subtle nor lacking in emotional intensity. However, during the meetings both Federn and Deutsch preserved the decorum that was appropriate in a scientific meeting.

In one of our meetings, an ugly scene took place between Siegfried Bernfeld and Robert Waelder. I have forgotten what the bone of contention was; I have a vague recollection that it concerned some theoretical question. But their arguments became increasingly heated, so everybody felt very uncomfortable. I feared the two might come to blows. However, this digression from the usual code of behavior in the meetings was a single event. I do not know whether a reconciliation later took place between the two adversaries.

Three of the younger group of members exerted a beneficial influence on the scientific level of the society: Robert Waelder, Ernst Kris, and Heinz Hartmann. Only Hartmann was trained as a physician. All three had solid backgrounds in epistemology and the methodology of the scientific process. Most of the other members of the society were medical doctors whose training did not include any methodology of science. Their approach, particularly in applying analysis to art and literature, was often naive and dilletantish. The discussions by Waelder, Kris, and Hartmann were conducted on a higher level of methodological correctness. Their remarks and methodological criticism raised the level of scientific thinking of all of the members.

IV. Developments of the Late 1920s and the 1930s

CHANGES IN THE VIENNA PSYCHOANALYTIC SOCIETY; INFLUENCES OF OTHER COUNTRIES

In the late twenties and early thirties the society lost a number of valuable members. I have described how miserable the economic situation in Austria had become during World War I. After a relatively short recovery in the midtwenties, the situation deteriorated again, while in neighboring Germany the economy improved and the catastrophic inflation of the early twenties was replaced by monetary stability. The more favorable economic conditions in Germany and the intense cultural life, particularly in Berlin, lured many Austrian scientists and artists to emigrate to Germany. Some of the members of the Vienna Psychoanalytic Society followed this trend. Otto Fenichel was the first to emigrate to Berlin in 1923. Siegfried Bernfeld followed him. Soon Theodor Reik left for Berlin, and so did René Spitz.

There were also theoretical disagreements that caused two important members of the Vienna psychoanalytic community, Otto Rank and Wilhelm Reich, to leave. For a period of two decades, Otto Rank had been one of the most productive contributors to the new science and Freud had had a special affection for him. Rank had kept very careful minutes of the society since its foundation in 1908. He had a profound intuitive understanding of the mode of functioning of the primary process which enabled him to find the hidden meaning in mental manifestations, from relatively unimportant but revealing slip actions to the highest works of creativity. To the variety of clinical and therapeutic subjects on which he wrote he added analytical explorations of works of world literature which demonstrate his wide knowledge. His mental agility and excellent writing style make reading his work an exquisite pleasure. In my opinion, his most important work is *Das Inzestmotiv in Dichtung und Sage* (The incest motif in poetry and saga), which was published in 1912. In it he surveyed world literature and proved the ubiquity of the Oedipus complex. Rank's ingenious flair for the unconscious led him to discover the hidden Oedipal significance in a multitude of novels, short stories, and plays. He wrote this book at Freud's suggestion. Thus, it is all the more amazing that an undissolved antagonism toward Freud, who was obviously a father image, expressed itself in a negative attitude toward Freud's most fundamental discoveries, particulary the Oedipal complex.

This radical change in Rank's attitude occurred around 1923. Helene Deutsch told me that during a small party she gave in that year to honor Rank's fortieth birthday, Rank remarked that now that he was forty years old, it was time for a change in his life.* After the publication of his book *The Trauma of Birth* and after Freud's negative reaction to the theory of anxiety that Rank developed in the book, Rank broke his connection with Freud and with the Vienna society. My speculation, even at that time, was that Rank had been anticipating that Freud would die of cancer soon after the discovery of his illness in 1923. Rank had hoped that his own theory of anxiety related to the birth trauma would make him the new leader of the psychoanalytic movement. When Freud did not die, and when he found Rank's new theory of anxiety unacceptable, Rank reacted with a rebellious separation from Freud and his science, to which he had formerly make such valuable contributions. He left Vienna for Paris in 1925 and later emigrated to Philadelphia. He broke with Freud and psychoanalysis completely, and devoted his efforts to disproving Freud's basic findings.

Wilhelm Reich exchanged his Vienna battlefield for Berlin early in the 1930s. Analysis had lost him before this move, however, because of his unacceptable theoretical and technical ideas and because of trouble that his increasing characterological diffi-

---

*In ancient Rome, with whose literature Rank was thoroughly familiar, an adolescent became a *vir* (man) at forty.

culties created in the psychoanalytic community. Reich had become more and more rigid in his technical approach. In his later writings, he postulated a strict regularity of the appearance of resistances in the course of treatment which, according to his view, made a systematized interpretative approach to resistances necessary. This regulation of the technical procedure inhibited the flexibility and open mindedness so necessary in the analyst's approach to the patient. In addition, Reich became more and more sadistic in "hammering" at the patient's resistive armor. An increasing number of the members and trainees in the seminars could not follow him and had to contradict his technical advice, a fact that made him embittered and belligerent. Even Freud could not tolerate Reich's stubborn insistance on his being right. In one of the meetings in Freud's apartment which I attended, Freud stopped Reich's righteous repetition of his argument by not permitting him to continue his discussion.

Another unacceptable theory of Wilhelm Reich's which he pursued with increasing fanaticism was his conviction that a perfect orgasm will prevent or cure any form of neurosis. Freud himself pointed out to Reich in one of the meetings at the Berggasse 19, the fact that many neurosogenic drives, particularly pregenital ones, cannot be discharged, even by the most perfect orgasm. The general observation that some neurotics, particularly compulsives, can have impeccable orgasms without being cured by them did not make any inroad on Reich's conviction concerning the healing and preventive function of orgasm. He stubbornly stuck to his ideas. Mockingly we younger analysts spoke of Reich's "genital paradise." In my opinion, he defended his thesis so rigorously because his character corresponded very much to the "genital narcissist," which he so well described in one of his papers.

I think Reich drew the thesis of the mental hygenic influence of orgasm out of his own experience. He told me once that if he did not have an orgasm for two days, he felt physically unwell and "saw black before his eyes" like before an approaching spell of fainting. These symptoms disappeared immediately with an orgasmic experience. However, his orgasms, which he described as paradigmatic, prevented neither his increasing character pathology nor his final psychotic manifestation.

In the midtwenties, Editha and I had befriended Wilhelm and Annie Reich. The four of us went on excursions through the Vienna woods, on one-day skiing trips in the nearest high mountains south of Vienna (like Rax and Schneeberg, which were about six thousand feet above sea level and offered very good trails down into the valley). In the summer of 1928, we visited the Reichs during their vacation on a Carinthian lake, and stayed with them for a few days. Once, in spring of 1932, we went together with a tourist group for a week to Davos in Switzerland and Wilhelm Reich and I skied down the famous Parsenn trail. On the way down, I fell once, Reich three times. He was visibly furious that I turned out to be the better skier. By this time, his pathological character traits had become obvious to all who had contact with him. His friends became more and more concerned about his aggressive and unyielding behavior. We also could not agree with his radical political ideas. We tried to persuade him to enter a therapeutic analysis again (he had been analyzed by Dr. Paul Federn, but he never had anything positive to say about his work with Federn). We suggested that he should have more analysis with Sandor Ferenczi in Budapest, whose reputation as a brilliant therapist was acknowledged by all of us. (Helene Deutsch said once to me, "Ferenczi could cure even a horse.") Instead, Reich left Vienna for Berlin and went to Sandor Rado for therapy, but he broke off the therapy after a short while. His ideas developed more and more into delusions like his orgone theory, and psychoanalysis lost him for good. His tragic ending in prison in the United States is well known. I always felt that his development away from scientific psychoanalysis and classical technique was a real loss. It meant for me also the personal loss of an excellent teacher, a friend, and, when I was starting out, a promoter of my analytic career. As I have described, he had offered me his supervision after my first case report in his seminar and later, after I presented my first technical paper at his seminar, he offered me the position on the staff of the psychoanalytic outpatient clinic. He also had sent me my first private patient for analysis.

I argued once in a society meeting against Reich's systematization of resistance analysis. He became pale with anger and rage and bit his lips when I contradicted his theory. He did not accept my arguments, and he was very disappointed that I did not follow him. I felt bad that the argument coming from me hurt him deeply. He certainly must have considered me disloyal, but I felt incapable of being scientifically dishonest and I had found his trend of development unacceptable. I was not the only one, because not one member of the society stayed with him in his deviation, not even his wife, Annie, who left him and became an important psychoanalytic research worker and contributor to our science independent from him. His separation from the society in Vienna was gradual. By 1934, when he came to the International Congress in Lucerne, Switzerland, he did not participate in the meetings either scientifically or socially. From what I heard, he stayed in a tent with a girlfriend.

When Reich left Vienna, Helene Deutsch took over the technical seminar, which she conducted from 1932 until 1935. The seminar remained most instructive but its character changed radically. Helene Deutsch focused much more on the understanding of the unconscious meaning of the material brought forth by the patient than on technique. She perceived the unconscious significance of the patient's material with an amazing acuity; she had the most sensitive "third ear."[*] Equally amazing was her ability to predict what would follow in the next phase of the therapy. Her keen intuitive understanding of the primary process gave unexpected meaning to seemingly insignificant details as well as bizarre-appearing manifestations.

Helene Deutsch held the seminar in her apartment in the inner city, the oldest section of Vienna. She worked until late in the evening with her patients—she was then very much in demand as a training analyst, particularly by American students of the institute—therefore she started the seminar at 9:30 P.M. In general, more than one case was reported, which was very tiring for all of us. Not infrequently, Helene Deutsch asked for the report of another case at 1:00 A.M. We all were near exhaustion and she herself often sat with closed eyes, seemingly half asleep. However, all of a sudden she would become alive and give a brilliant exposé of the analytic situation. It was almost uncanny how

[*]Theodor Reik, *Listening with the Third Ear: The Inner Experience of a Psychoanalyst* (New York: Farrar, Straus, 1948).

she divined unconscious meaning and trend from the trainees' often rather poor report. Her discussion woke everyone up and we left her apartment newly stimulated, sometimes after 2 A.M. On our walk home—the streetcars had long since stopped running—we were filled with admiration for Helene Deutsch's ingenious insights. But she hardly ever uttered a sentence about the technique of using the recognized unconscious meaning and how to approach the patient's resistance, something that had been Wilhelm Reich's great strength. What we had learned of technique from Reich presented the complement to Deutsch's brilliant understanding. The combination of what we learned from these two teachers provided a perfect clinical therapeutic education.

By 1935, when I was already an analyst with ten years of experience, I gave a continuous report on a difficult case in the seminar. It was amazing even for me how Helene Deutsch could draw conclusions concerning the unconscious dynamic undercurrents in the reported material, and I could only marvel at her ability to recognize unconscious transference trends from very scanty indications in the patient's material.

During the period when Helene Deutsch conducted the seminar, two trainees who would become outstanding figures in psychoanalysis reported on their first cases. One was Erik Erikson and the other was Ernest Kris. Neither was a medical doctor. At this early point one could already recognize their outstanding psychological insight and their rapidly growing skill in the technique of therapy.

After Helene Deutsch left Vienna for the United States in 1935, the seminar was conducted by Hermann Nunberg, Edward Bibring, Grete Bibring, me, and finally Anna Freud (I do not remember the exact sequence). I think during the last month of the existence of the institute, Anna Freud conducted the technical seminar regularly.*

I attended the technical seminar for twelve years. Besides the technical papers of Sigmund Freud, I owe the seminar a solid foundation of clinical insight and technical experience. Three of

---

*My memories partially differ from the report on the technical seminar by Hans Lobner in *Sigmund Freud House Bulletin* 2, no. 2 (1978): 16.

my clinical-therapeutic papers grew out of my experience in these seminars. The first, "On Latent Negative Transference," my graduation paper from the institute, I entirely owe to Wilhelm Reich's teaching. After it appeared in *Internationale Zeitschrift fuer Psychoanalyse*, it found the approval of Ernest Jones, who made some positive remarks about it to me when I introduced myself to him at the International Psychoanalytic Congress in Innsbruck in 1927.

The second paper, "The Dynamics of the Dissolution of the Transference Resistance," was presented in a society meeting early in 1929. It is also based on what I learned from Wilhelm Reich.

The third paper, entitled "The Fate of the Ego in Psychoanalytic Therapy," I presented in 1932 to the International Psychoanalytic Congress in Wiesbaden. Again it was based on the dynamic understanding of the therapeutic process that I had acquired in the technical seminar. After the presentation of this paper at the International Congress, Paul Federn took violent exception to my concept of the "therapeutic split" of the ego. He did this when he saw me after the meeting in a restaurant, where Editha and I were enjoying some coffee with our friends Dr. and Mrs. Behn-Eschenburg, an analytic couple from Zurich. They were appalled by what they considered insulting remarks by Federn. I had to explain to them that such stormy expressions were natural to Federn's impulsive character and that I did not feel offended by his disapproval.

It was the custom of the Vienna society to have the members present their Congress papers again at society meetings for more general discussion. When I presented "The Fate of the Ego in Psychoanalytic Therapy" in the Vienna society in the fall of 1932, the storm of indignation and rejection concerning the term *ego split* in therapy was as strong as Federn's had been in Wiesbaden. Particularly Hermann Nunberg, Paul Federn again, Helene Deutsch, and Ludwig Jekels objected strenuously. Only Anna Freud said that she did not understand the objections to a concept that to her thinking, dealt correctly with an important factor in the dynamic process of therapy.

Shortly after I presented my congress paper at a Vienna Psychoanalytic Society meeting, Freud's *New Series of Introductory*

Lectures was published. In it Freud says in chapter 31, "Dissection of the Personality": "The ego can take itself as an object, can treat itself like other objects, criticize itself, and do Heaven knows what with itself. In this, one part of the ego is setting itself over against the rest. So the ego can be split; it splits itself during a number of its functions—temporarily at least. Its parts can come together again afterwards" (Standard Edition, vol. 22, p. 58).

In one of the succeeding society meetings I quoted the above sentences to justify the concept of therapeutic ego split in therapy which I had established in my paper. Ludwig Jekels answered in a very authoritarian and somewhat contemptuous tone that the criticism of my paper in the last meeting had not been directed to the concept of the ego split but was an expression of the general opinion that the paper was trivial and presented only platitudes. There was no further discussion, because Otto Fenichel, the main speaker at this meeting, arrived. His train from Berlin had been late. I had taken the opportunity to present my vindication of my concept of the ego split while the assembly was waiting for Fenichel's arrival.

Since then, the paper has been generally accepted. In fact, the two concepts of the "therapeutic ego split" and the "therapeutic alliance," which I established therein, have become household terms in the psychoanalytic literature on the dynamics of the therapeutic process. "Habent sua fata libelli" (little books [and papers] have their own fate).

The loss of Fenichel, Bernfeld, Reik, and the others in the 1920s was noticeable, but there was such a wealth of excellent analytic thinkers left, and new ones were coming out of the institute, that the society continued to flourish with scientific productivity.

The Viennese analysts formed a tightly knit group. We lived in more or less hostile surroundings. In academic circles, psychoanalysis was not considered a serious science. I have spoken of the animosity of other psychiatrists toward psychoanalysis. The medical profession in general refused to acknowledge psychoanalysis as a discipline worthy of recognition. Professor Karl Buehler, then head of the Department of Psychology at the University of Vienna, and his wife, Charlotte, an associate professor in her husband's department, were reluctant to recognize the importance of Freud's discoveries. The Catholic church, a mighty power in Austria, was an embittered enemy of psychoanalysis. Pater Wilhelm Schmidt, the editor of *Anthropos*, the most important Catholic periodical in anthropology, was an ethnologist of international renown in Catholic circles. He expressed the most hostile disapproval of Freud and analysis in many of his publications. Rudolf Allers, M.D. and Ph.D., a Jew converted to Catholicism, an "individual psychologist" belonging to the circle of Alfred Adler, relentlessly and viciously attacked psychoanalysis in his writings and lectures. The leading Catholic newspaper, *Reichspost*, never missed an opportunity to denigrate and condemn psychoanalysis. Particularly when Freud's *Future of an Illusion* was published in 1927, a violent campaign against Freud and psychoanalysis was launched by the Catholic church as well as by other religious groups. In addition, the strength that the right-wing political elements derived from Mussolini's dominance in Italy and from the rising power of National Socialism increased the hostility against psychoanalysis. When Freud expressed doubts about Marxism because of its lack of psychological consideration in *New Series of Introductory Lectures* in 1933, the Marxist camp joined the enemies of psychoanalysis.

One of the most read and most feared Viennese writers, the satirist and social critic Karl Kraus, who was widely read in intellectual circles, regularly mocked psychoanalysis with acrimony in his publication *Die Fackel* (the torch). Although he had no real understanding of what psychoanalysis was, no witty aperçu was too cheap if he could use it to express his hatred of the *psychoanalen*, as he called psychoanalysts, referring to the recognition of the anal phase in psychosexual development. His statement "Psychoanalysis is the sickness which it pretends to heal" was just one of his many invectives. We analysts could not help feeling that we were working in a hostile camp. But Freud's strength of spirit and his conviction that scientific truth will prevail helped us to go on working, unshaken by the multifaceted opposition to analysis in Austria. In intellectual circles, which were not committed to an ideology inimical to psychoanalysis, Freud and his science were mostly ignored. Even in the twenties, well-educated people were often completely oblivious to the existence of the great man among them and unaware of his work.

All this more or less isolated the analytic community from the cultural strata of Viennese society. Analysts were frequently met with mistrust and suspicion or ridicule in social situations. It was natural that we established social ties and personal friendships among our colleagues. A remarkable number of us found our spouse within our group: Edward and Grete Bibring, Wilhelm and Annie Reich, Willy and Hedwig Hoffer, Richard and Editha Sterba, Robert and Jenny Waelder, Ernst and Marianne Kris, and Otto and Melitta Sperling. With the exception of Waelder's and Reich's, these marriages were of unusual permanence. The conjugal ties between Otto Isakower and Salomea Guttmann, although established only in the emigration, grew out of the closeness of the members of the Vienna group. Friendships between members led to common social and sportive activities, like Sunday hikes in the Vienna Woods, ski excursions into the Austrian and Swiss Alps, visits in the vacation places, rubber boat trips on the Danube and its tributaries, and Sunday outings to the Danube beaches. We had a wonderful time together.

During this period, a number of works were published in the field of child analysis, a important benefit of the Kinderseminars started in 1926. Anna Freud's book *Technique of Child Analysis* (1927) was the first and most valuable result. A series of Editha's papers which were published in the 1930s resulted from her work with children reported on in this seminar. The most important, "An Abnormal Child," was the account of her treatment of an autistic child. It appeared in 1933 in *Zeitschrift fuer Psychoanalytische Paedagogik* and in 1936 in English in *Psychoanalytic Quarterly*. "Analysis of Psychogenic Constipation in a Two-Year-Old Child" (1934) and several other papers of this period were reports on the analytic treatment of children which she had presented in Anna Freud's seminar.

The summer and fall of 1927 hold many happy memories for us. Helene Deutsch had rented an apartment in Editha's family's villa in Gmunden on lake Traunsee during the summer vacation, and she and her son Martin stayed with us for almost four weeks. Her husband, Felix, drove by car from Vienna to spend the weekends with his family. It was the first car he had purchased, a Steyr-Sedan, and he was very proud of it. The Deutsch family and Editha and I made motor trips to several of the beautiful lakes which are dispersed in the Salzkammergut; the weather was perfect that summer. Helene Deutsch enjoyed this vacation so much that in Gmunden she wrote her paper for the International Congress that was to take place in September 1927 in Innsbruck. Her subject corresponded to her joyful vacation mood: "Uber Zufriedenheit, Glück und Ekstase" (Happiness, contentment, and ecstasy). *

Our vacations ended with a delightful experience, the International Congress in Innsbruck. This congress was attended by approximately three hundred members (in 1924 at the Salzburg congress there had been only seventy). The beautiful medieval city of Innsbruck, with the towering mountain range of the north chain of the Alps, showed itself at its best under three days of cloudless skies with brilliant sunshine. According to my memory, we Viennese members felt unusually close to each other, particularly one free afternoon during which, in the most carefree mood, we played children's games on a meadow. The Deutschs, many of our group, my wife, and I participated.

The summer in Gmunden had brought us closer to Helene and Felix Deutsch, and several times during the following fall they took us in their car into the beautiful environs of Vienna. These trips were a real treat, for cars were still a rarity at that time. No analyst had a car, not even Sigmund Freud or Anna. The only ones in possession of a car in the twenties were Mrs. Dorothy Tiffany-Burlingham and Max Schur. I think that later, in the thirties, Heinz Hartmann had a car. In the city the streetcars and buses provided convenient transportation. Taxis were not beyond our reach once we had private patients. In the inner city everything was in walking distance, so a car was not a necessity. Besides, the possession of a car immediately put one into a higher tax bracket. The Austrian internal revenue service demanded no exact income declaration. The amount of taxes was estimated according to one's living quarters and standard of living, and a car was considered a luxury. My wife and I learned to drive a car only after our immigration to the United States.

For a Viennese group there were conspicuously few amateur musicians among the members. (One reason for this may have

Internationale Zeitschrift fuer Psychoanalyse 13 (1927): 410-19.

been that many of them had not grown up in Vienna.) Besides me, there was Felix Deutsch, who played the piano; he was very good at sight reading. For a while he and a cellist who was not an analyst and I, a violinist, played classical piano trios, usually Haydn and Mozart; we rarely tackled Beethoven. We played at the Deutschs' apartment. Helene Deutsch was our audience, and she was often joined by Beata Rank. Princess Marie Bonaparte also attended a few times. But in the "city of music," where in many families chamber music and particularly string quartets was an important and regular activity, the analytic group was musically impoverished.

During the thirties, Editha gave birth to two children, both girls. The pregnancies, the children's arrival, and their development enriched our lives. We were a very happy family. During the infancy and early years of our older daughter, Dr. Margret Schoenberger was our pediatrician. Dr. Schoenberger, who published under her married name, Mahler, received world-wide recognition for her studies of early childhood development. As pediatrician for our daughter, she insisted that the baby be weighed before and after every breastfeeding to determine the exact quantity of nourishment taken, a procedure not uncommon during the period of breastfeeding. She was very conscientious and exacting, and always saw the child on housecalls; our daughter thrived under her care. When our second daughter was born three years after the first, Dr. Schoenberger was too occupied with her analytic work, and we had to change to another pediatrician.

After 1 March 1933, when Hitler came to power in the German Reich, the migratory flood, which had taken several of our colleagues to Germany, reversed its course. Some of the Viennese members who had left for Berlin during the 1920s returned to Vienna when the Nazi regime was established in Germany: Siegfried Bernfeld, René Spitz, and Theodor Reik. The impossibility of continuing analysis in Germany in the absence of freedom of thought and speech, and the persecution of the Jews forced many of the German analysts into emigration. The move to Vienna was the easiest change, particularly because of the common language. The Viennese analysts received the returning former members as well as the newcomers with open arms. We felt that their addition was an enrichment of and a stimulus for the activities of the society and the institute.

The influx of new ideas and influences brought by the new-comers—particularly Hanns Lampl and his wife, Jeanne Lampl de Groot, and Berta Bornstein—contributed much to the society meetings. Some of the trainees of the Berlin Institute came to Vienna to continue and complete their training, among them some who later became *personnages en vue* in the analytic scene, such as Paul Kramer, Anna Maennchen, and H. Winnik. Otto Fenichel, who settled in Prague, contributed indirectly to the enrichment of our Viennese group. He established an analytic training center in Prague, where he was joined by Annie Reich and by Steffi Bornstein, Bertha Bornstein's sister. Emanuel Windholz emerged from the Prague group. The Vienna Society was enriched by the Prague analytic community through frequent visits to Vienna by the Prague analysts. Otto Fenichel's contributions were most stimulating. Prague was much closer to Vienna than Berlin (the distance was only a few hours' train ride), which made guest lectures easy. Editha and I presented papers to the Prague group.

Vienna, Budapest, Prague, and Rome were near enough to suggest the idea of annual meetings of the respective analytic communities in these cities in the form of *Vierlaendertagungen* (four-country meetings). The fourth constituent country for the meetings was supposed to be Italy, where Eduardo Weiss had been active as an analytic pioneer, first in Trieste (which until 1918 belonged to Austria) and after 1918 in Rome, where he founded a psychoanalytic group with Nicola Perrotti and Emilio Servadio. However, I do not remember any Italian psychoanalysts ever participating in the meetings. Only two such meetings took place before 1938. The first convened in the spring of 1935 in Vienna. It was well attended, the interest was intense, and the participants were satisfied with the project. In 1937 the meeting took place in the spring in Budapest. I attended both meetings. I felt the memories of the historically unifying role of the Austro-Hungarian empire contributed to the camaraderie among the colleagues from the different parts of the monarchy. At least in me the meeting awoke nostalgic feelings for the glory of the Habsburg empire, which had ended with such an unhappy and unfortunate dismemberment.

At the first *Vierlaendertagung* in Vienna in 1935 I spoke on the last technical papers by Ferenczi. The Hungarian colleagues seemed to be pleased with my presentation, which, although it was not uncritical of his latest technical attempts, paid homage to Ferenczi's unusual human kindness and his fertile scientific creativity. Anna Freud told me afterward that my presentation made one realize that Ferenczi's last papers were the outcome of his sickness. She said: "When one heard your presentation, one had to realize that it was a case history." The paper, "The Psychic Trauma and the Handling of the Transference: The Last Contributions of S. Ferenczi to Psychoanalytic Technique," was published in *Internationale Zeitschrift fuer Psychoanalyse* in 1936. The mood during the meeting and in the evenings was one of camaraderie and cheerfulness. At the meeting I met many of the Hungarian colleagues for the first time. They had known me only from my publications and several of them expressed their surprise at my youthful appearance.

My memories of the second Vierlaendertagung in Budapest are much dimmer, I think, because it was my first visit to Budapest, the second capital of the old monarchy. Its beautiful setting on both banks of the Danube River was so different from that of Vienna, which lies at a distance from the Danube (only a branch of the river flows through the northeastern part of the city). Sightseeing and museum visits in Budapest detracted from my attendance at the meetings.

When Hitler came into Austria in 1938, these regional meetings had to be given up.

The membership and the attendance at the meetings of the Vienna Society had swelled considerably during the late twenties and early thirties, as the institute gained recognition and graduated an increasing number of trainees. The at least spiritual presence of Freud and the concentration of brilliant minds in the Mecca of psychoanalysis attracted many analysts and students from foreign countries (particularly the United States) who sought to enlarge their theoretical knowledge and improve their technical skill. After the abolishment of the Berlin Society and institute in 1933, Vienna was the most important center of psychoanalysis until it fell to the Nazis in 1938. Previously Berlin rivaled Vienna as a center for psychoanalytic study.

Among the Americans who came to Vienna for training and studies were Ruth Mack-Brunswick, Dorothy Tiffany-Burlingham, Sidney G. Biddle, Hyman Lippman, Ralph Kaufman, Estelle Levy, Molly Putnam, Edith B. Jackson, Margaret Fries, Julia Deming, Leroy Maeder, John Dorsey, Muriel Gardner, and Helen Tartakoff. They were warmly welcomed by the analytic group, and the faculty of the institute made every effort to give the students the best training. The language of the institute was German exclusively, but the faculty, myself included, offered private instruction in English to the American trainees.

The gratitude and loyalty of the Americans to the Vienna analysts expressed itself in their splendid efforts to help their Viennese teachers and colleagues after the destruction of the Vienna Society and institute. They provided affidavits of support for their Viennese colleagues which were needed to obtain immigration visas to the United States and generously helped the analyst refugees to establish themselves in American cities. Many permanent friendships between the foreign analysts and trainees and their Viennese colleagues developed. In the thirties, the close international analytic community in Vienna included American, British, French, Dutch, Swiss, Swedish, Yugoslavian, Polish, and Spanish analysts or trainees.

In 1931, at the suggestion of A. J. Storfer, I had undertaken the task of writing a psychoanalytic dictionary *(Handwörterbuch der Psychoanalyse)*. Storfer actually began this work with the definition of a few terms beginning with the letter A, but he found the task too time consuming. He asked me to continue the work with him, to which I agreed. It was a project for which my experience in 1925 and 1926, working on the index of the *Gesammelte Schriften von Sigmund Freud* (Collected works of Sigmund Freud) was an enormous help. Soon, however, Storfer lost interest in or courage for the enormous project and dropped out of our partnership. As ransom for dissolving the partnership, he gave me the index galleys and typescript pages and all of the eleven volumes of the *Gesamtausgabe.* I carried on the work alone. The dictionary was supposed to appear gradually in sixteen issues, of which the first was published on the occasion of Freud's eightieth birthday, 6 May 1936.

The preface to the first issue was the facsimile of a letter Sigmund Freud wrote to me. When I had finished the letter A of the dictionary, I had given a copy to Anna Freud and asked her to submit it for Freud's scrutiny. After a short while I received this letter from Freud, which I quote here in English translation.

> Your "Dictionary" gives me the impression of being a valuable aid to learners and of being a fine achievement on its own account. The precision and correctness of the individual entries is in fact of commendable excellence. English and French translations of the headings are not indispensable but would add further to the value of the work. I do not overlook the fact that the path from the letter A to the end of the alphabet is a very long one, and that to follow it would mean an enormous burden of work for you. So do not do it unless you feel an internal obligation—only obey a compulsion of that kind and certainly not any external pressure.
>
> Yours sincerely,
> Freud[*]

James Strachey, the translator of the letter, added a footnote: "The letter was written when the work had only just been started and when Freud had only seen a sample of it."

When I sent Freud, on the occasion of his eightieth birthday, the first printed issue of the dictionary, he wrote me a short note expressing his satisfaction that the publication coincided with his birthday. In addition, he sent me the rarely published photograph reproduced here. He had received as a birthday gift the fountain-

---

[*]This translation by James Strachey of the original German letter appears in volume 22 of the standard edition of *The Complete Psychological Works of Sigmund Freud*. The translations mentioned by Freud were, in fact, included in the finished work. The translation of the terms into English was made by Dr. Edith B. Jackson of Vienna with the support of the English Glossary Committee under the direction of Dr. Ernest Jones of London. The translation of the terms into French was made by La Commission Linguistique pour Vocabulaire Psychoanalytique Français of Paris under the direction of Dr. Eduard Pichon, president, and Princess Marie Bonaparte, vice-president.

pen with which he signed it. The ink spot on the picture I owe to his new pen. The card, written by Freud in longhand, unfortunately got lost during my emigration.

Four subsequent issues of the dictionary appeared in the following two years, until the occupation of Austria by the Germans brought the undertaking to an end. The last term discussed in the fifth volume is *Groessenwahn* (megalomania), and it remains undecided whether the ending of the work with the word *megalomania* refers to my megalomania or to Hitler's. I did not find the courage to continue, or rather to start, the undertaking in English. German-speaking people find the beginning of the work still useful; when I met Adolf Meyer in the United States, he urged me to continue the dictionary because he found it so helpful. I consider it indicative of the spirit and enthusiasm for the cause in which all members of the Viennese group of analysts participated that as a single individual I had the courage to undertake such an enormous task. However, even though I did not finish it, I acquired a vast knowledge, particularly of Freud's writings, and I still profit from the effort.

V. Freud Himself*

For the first three years of my association with the Vienna Psychoanalytic Society, Sigmund Freud was not present at the meetings because of his prolonged illness. There were only two occasions when Freud was in direct contact with our group. The first was the mourning session for Karl Abraham, early in January 1926; the second, Freud's seventieth birthday, 6 May 1926.

On 6 January 1926, the society held a memorial meeting for Karl Abraham, who had died on Christmas Day of 1925. From 1923 until the dissolution of the society in March 1938, this was the only official meeting that Freud attended. I saw him for the first time on this occasion. The meeting took place in the lecture room of the Herzstation. It was set for 9:00 P.M. Freud entered the room with his daughter, Anna, at the exact time. He wore a *Stadtpelz* (a fur-lined, rather lengthy overcoat with a broad collar of dark fur), a typical piece of winter clothing for gentlemen of the upper classes. He was smaller in stature than I had expected. I cannot say whether it was my preconceived idea of him or some aura that he radiated that made me feel that we were in the presence of an outstanding personality. His presence immediately dominated the scene although he uttered only a few words. When Freud entered the lecture room, the assembly rose. Freud removed his coat and took his place at the head of the rectangular table. Anna sat on his left. We all sat down in silence, waiting for Theodor Reik, the main speaker, who had not yet arrived. When Reik stormed into the room three or four minutes later, Freud

*A portion of this chapter appeared in my article "Discussions of Sigmund Freud," *Psychoanalytic Quarterly* 47 (1978): 173-91, and is included here by permission.

spoke to him with a sharp tone of voice: "We were thinking you would not come any more." Even in the presence of Freud, Reik played the role of the black sheep of the group; Reik must have known very well how strictly Freud always insisted upon punctuality. Then Anna Freud read her father's short address, which ended with the highest praise for Karl Abraham's character, expressed in Latin, which Freud loved so much. Freud applied to Abraham Horace's well-known verse: "Integer Vitae scelerisque purus" (unstained in life and pure from any vice). About Reik's speech I have kept no memory, probably because I was too preoccupied with absorbing Freud's presence.

Freud's seventieth birthday was 6 May 1926. He felt well enough to receive the members of the society and the trainees of the institute in his home. It was then that I was introduced to and shook hands with the man who was of such importance to me and to the world. It was my birthday, too, but I mainly celebrated Freud's handshake. Freud's apartment was filled with flowers, particularly anthuriums, which were among his favorite. I took one of his cigars—there were many boxes of different kinds of cigars standing around in the rooms which were open to the guests—but I did not light it. I kept it as a souvenir, and smoked it sometime later on a special occasion.

Although we missed having personal contact with Freud, his presence was felt as an inspiring force. His spirit dominated the group. In addition, Anna Freud provided a direct link to the master. It was always impressive when she said: "Mein Vater hat gesagt . . ." (my father has said . . .), although it was a rare occurrence.

We all knew of Freud's cancer, and his sickness was a constant worry for us. We knew very few of the details and only occasionally did some news of his condition seep through to us from one of his analysands whose treatment had to be interrupted because of a temporary worsening of Freud's health. Occasionally we heard something about the removal of a new leukoplakial lesion, and were relieved every time we found out that Freud had taken up his work with patients again. I was deeply shocked when I read many years later in Ernest Jones's biography the detailed report that Freud's oral surgeon, Professor Pichler, kept on the Freud case. What an ordeal Freud had to go through over a

period of seventeen years, while his extraordinary scientific productivity remained undiminished! He suffered through thirty-one
operations, mainly to remove leukoplakias that developed again
and again in the region where Pichler had performed the radical
surgery. The biopsies regularly showed a tendency to malignant
growths and, according to the pathologist, Professor Erdheim,
they were caused by Freud's addiction to cigar smoking. Every
surgical procedure was in itself very unpleasant, but the operations were always followed by periods of intense pain; after each
operation the prosthesis had to be put in immediately to prevent
scar formation from shrinking.

Not once had Max Schur, Freud's personal physician at that
time and a good friend of ours, told us anything about these epi-
sodes, which must have put a heavy burden of responsibility on
him. However, Josef Weinmann, another close friend of ours, who
was Freud's dentist and had participated in the construction of
the prosthesis, told me of an event that took place after Freud had
undergone approximately nine operations. Professor Pichler had
discovered another leukoplakia, which showed up on the X-ray,
and he had informed Freud of the need for another operation.
Freud refused to be operated on again and declared that he had
decided to let the cancerous growth take its course of destruction.
Professor Pichler suggested a consultation with professor Guido
Holzknecht, the top radiologist in Vienna. Holzknecht had begun
to work with X-rays before their destructive effect on living tis-
sues was recognized. For years he had exposed his hands and arms
unprotected to the deadly rays, and multiple cancer growths had
developed that had to be removed surgically, so his upper
extremities were greatly mutilated. His general health had
already deteriorated so much that he was hospitalized at the time
when Pichler suggested that consultation with him. Pichler,
Freud, and Weinmann went to the hospital were Holzknecht was
an inpatient, and Pichler showed Holzknecht the X-ray of Freud's
new lesion. After Holzknecht had examined the plate, he said:
"Freud, you have to be operated on," to which Freud repeated
his refusal to undergo a tenth operation. Holzknecht simply
remarked: "What should I say? I will be operated on tomorrow for
the twenty-fifth time." Then the conversation turned to other,
unrelated matters. After the three visitors left Holzknecht's sick-

room, Freud said to Pichler and Weinmann: "We have visited a real hero. Of course, I will be operated on tomorrow." Freud lived and worked for many years after this episode.

The reader can well imagine what a great event it was for all of us when Dr. Paul Federn announced at the beginning of the winter of 1928 that Freud felt well enough to participate in scientific meetings with a very reduced number of members (twelve) in his office on Berggasse 19. The members of the Vorstand, the executive board of the society, were ex officio regular participants. A few other members of the society were selected by Federn to be admitted. Federn invited me repeatedly to be present, and I attended approximately ten of them; they took place sporadically between the years 1928 and 1932, with Freud presiding. They were planned as monthly events, but Freud's precarious health and his occasional relapses caused extensive interruptions in the schedule, so altogether not more than fifteen or twenty actually took place. The group met in the waiting room of Freud's office, which was relatively small. The board members and guests were already assembled when, at exactly 9:00 P.M., Freud would enter through the door that led to the waiting room from his treatment room and study. It was a most exciting experience to be in the presence of Freud, who was so much the central figure in our professional life.

The construction of the prosthesis in his mouth cavity was finally so successful that Freud could speak clearly. I never noticed any disturbance in his speech. His facial configuration seemed to me completely restored. His demeanor was alert and lively, the movement of his hands quick and assertive. However, when he sat silently in the meetings listening to the presentations and to the discussants, he often touched an area of his upper jaw with his fingers as if this gave him some relief from pain or discomforting pressure. He would then reach for another cigar from the box that stood before him on the table, clip it with a silver cigar clipper that was attached to a large curved ivory handle in the form of a horn, and light it with visible delight. I noted a peculiar feature in his posture: he liked to rest his left hand on his left shoulder.

For a psychoanalyst it was a unique event to hear Freud discuss various aspects of the science he had created, the science to which we had devoted our lives. I was therefore eager to retain as much as I possibly could of what he had to say to us. The best aid for such preservation would have been to write down all that Freud said, but we were told by Federn that the professor did not approve of taking notes at the meetings. However, I decided to be disobedient and to jot down as much as I could secretly, so that I could later reconstruct Freud's remarks from these notes. I could do this only if I sat in one of the chairs in the back, where neither the professor nor Federn could see me, and this was possible only a few times out of the approximately ten meetings that I attended.

The general structure of the meetings was as follows. During the first part, a member of the assembly either presented an original paper or reviewed the latest publication by Freud (*Inhibitions, Symptoms, and Anxiety,* "The Future of an Illusion," and *Civilization and Its Discontents* had all been published relatively recently). This was followed by a short discussion by the participants. In general, Freud made only a few minor remarks during this part of the meeting. Then there would be a short break, during which we took some refreshments. Needless to say, there were no alcoholic beverages. During this intermission, one had the opportunity to talk to Freud privately if he was not occupied with discussing society matters with Federn.

After the break, the meeting continued. During the second part, Freud participated much more in the discussion. At times he gave a lengthy elaboration of or an opinion on the subject. Once he spoke for almost half an hour. Unfortunately, I was not able to take notes, for I sat right across the table from him, since I had presented the paper under discussion. However, I remember a few of his remarks on that occasion, and I will report those later. You will note that in the official meetings of the Vienna Society, during which Otto Rank took careful minutes,* very often Freud also spoke extensively at the end of the meeting. However, there is a great difference between his discussions at the time of the official society meetings, which took place in the second half of the first

---

*The minutes from 1906 to 1918 are available as a four-volume set edited by Herman Nunberg and Ernst Federn, *Minutes of the Vienna Psychoanalytic Society* (New York: International Universities Press, 1962-75).

decade of this century, and the meetings twenty or more years later. In the earlier meetings, Freud spoke as the leading personality of a movement that was exposed to much hostility and that had to fight for recognition, if not for survival. This made it necessary for Freud to scrutinize every utterance. The very meticulous, official recordings of the meetings by Rank must also have caused Freud to weigh his pronouncements carefully. One can discern this attitude in the published minutes.

The situation in the meetings that I attended was quite different. These were not official meetings of the society; the discussions were informal and they were not supposed to be recorded. Psychoanalysis had established itself, and, though it was still a controversial subject, Freud was by then certain that his science was here to stay and to grow. Besides, he could be relaxed in the secure feeling that he was in a group of disciples *der Sache ergeben* (devoted to the cause), as he had said of Ernest Jones. This permitted him to speak "off the cuff," and his remarks were meant to be off the record. You will see from my report how very free Freud was in his expression; he often supported his comments with an anecdote or illustrated them with a joke, something you rarely find in Rank's minutes. I think it was the very prohibition of written records that enabled Freud to express himself so freely and to be relatively unconcerned with scientific responsibility for the content of his discussion.

In one of his recently published letters to Edoardo Weiss (1970), Freud expressed his opinion on how one should evaluate what I have preserved of his discussions: "Remarks made in unpublished discussions establish no claim at all." We should heed his admonition. By communicating what I recorded of Freud's discussions, I make the reader an accomplice in my act of disobedience, as it were. I think the reader should keep in mind that Freud's remarks in the meetings I attended were more or less of a casual nature. They cannot be taken as equal to his published scientific pronouncements, in which he used all the care and caution so characteristic of his written work.

On 9 December 1928, Theodor Reik reported on Freud's "The Future of an Illusion."[*] Freud found Reik's presentation too

[*]*Imago* (1928).

elegant. What Freud said then constituted a preliminary outline of a subject he was to elaborate four years later in his "New Introductory Lectures," namely, a critical review of the different *Weltanschauungen.** It might be advisable at this point to repeat the definition Freud published in 1932:

> "Weltanschauung" is, I am afraid, a specifically German concept, the translation of which into foreign languages might well raise difficulties. If I try to give you a definition of it, it is bound to seem clumsy to you. In my opinion, then, a "Weltanschauung" is an intellectual construction which solves all the problems of our existence uniformly on the basis of one overriding hypothesis, which, accordingly, leaves no question unanswered and in which everything that interests us finds its fixed place. It will easily be understood that the possession of a "Weltanschauung" of this kind is among the ideal wishes of human beings. Believing in it one can feel secure in life, one can know what to strive for, and how one can deal most expediently with one's emotions and interests.†

According to my notes, in Freud's discussion of Reik's review of "The Future of an Illusion," Freud said:

> The character of a *Weltanschauung* can be obtained only through a comparison with other *Weltanschauungen.* The scientific *Weltanschauung* is fragmentary and incomplete, but it is able to grow and to change. He who occupies himself with science arrives at agnosticism. Whoever relies on science gives up the demand for a well-defined unitarian structure. The totality is at present unrecognized. Five hundred years ago, a scientifically oriented person would have had to be completely pessimistic. We can only judge the present situation. We have to consider how young science is; it is not possible to know more than we do. Beyond this, everything is unknown. That is why the scientific *Weltanschauung* is of such a negative, incomplete, defective character.
>
> In contrast to this, other *Weltanschauungen* give a unified structure. What kinds of *Weltanschauungen* are

*Strachey's translation of *Weltanschauung* is "philosophy of life." I find the term "world view" more appropriate.

†*Standard Edition*, vol. 22.

there? There are: (1) the animistic, which still exists somewhere [Freud had written about it in *Totem and Taboo*]; (2) the religious, which also still exists, not only in Austria; (3) the materialistic, in which the Marxists believe, the so-called socialistic materialism; (4) the scientific, which renounces a general character; and (5) the mystic *Weltanschauung.*

Then Freud talked about the mystic *Weltanschauung:*

A great many cultured people who liberated themselves from religion adhere to this mystic *Weltanschauung.* Its essence is the high esteem of the irrational. The mystic *Weltanschauung* is the *Weltanschauung* of the future. Scholars, artists, and scientists embrace it and feel they have the right to look down on the other *Weltanschauungen.*

In comparison to the others, the scientific *Weltanschauung* is a poor Cinderella. The other *Weltanschauungen* believe in high values and distribute medals of distinction. In contrast to them, the scientific *Weltanschauung* is honest, it has nothing to give, and even that nothing is uncertain. The other *Weltanschauungen* have only contempt for the scientific, although they use it. Actually, they live only by it; otherwise, we would still be at the level of animism. At the same time, they insult it.

In turn, the scientific *Weltanschauung* cannot use anything of the others. It has the opportunity, however, to take revenge for the mistreatment, for science can *study* the other *Weltanschauungen.* And with this, the scientific *Weltanschauung* stops being harmless. The distinguished scholar will say, "Scientific explanation has no influence on the value system of a *Weltanschauung!*" However, in reality things are a little bit different.

To illustrate his point that scientific-psychological explanation destroys magical beliefs, Freud then told a fictitious story. For what follows it is significant to know that the German word for jaundice is *Gelbsucht* (yellow disease).

In the writings of Hippocrates there is mentioned a remedy against jaundice. Let us assume that at some university hospital this therapy is still taught, the professor and his staff believe in it, and it is regularly administered, with ambiguous results. The name of this medication is yellow turnips [*gelbe Rueben*—carrots]. Then along comes a young intern who is somewhat psychologically oriented, and he points out the possibility that the belief in the therapeutic effect of the yellow turnips in cases of yellow disease might be based on the common verbal element "yellow." You may be sure that the yellow turnip therapy will soon disappear. After the psychological connection is uncovered, the interest in this therapy is lost.

Religious persons will say that, even if explained psychologically, religious tenets might nevertheless be true. Yes, but only nevertheless. In reality, the yellow turnips arc finished. However, with the mystic *Weltanschauung*, a psychological explanation does not help. This one is the real enemy of the future. Our science is powerless against it. It is based on the belief in the irrational. People have a need to preserve a piece of mystic *Weltanschauung*. Parapsychologists try to transform the scientific into the mystic *Weltanschauung*.

It is my feeling that, to a great extent, it was the experience with Jung that made Freud so sensitive concerning mysticism and motivated him to express such grave concern about it. However, Freud has been right in his prophecy: the mystic *Weltanschauung* is indeed very widespread in present-day Western culture, and the high esteem of the irrational is constantly gaining ground, as we can easily observe.

I will have to make a few introductory remarks concerning the content of the next meeting at which I took some notes. The occasion was Wilhelm Reich's presentation of his thesis of the therapeutic and prophylactic effects of a perfect orgasm. Since the inhibition of genitality stems predominantly from the Oedipus complex, it was this nuclear complex of neurosis that Reich considered the archenemy of mental health.

It happened that at that time the Russians had undertaken a sociological experiment on the outcome of which they had set great hopes: it was supposed to mold the young generation from the start for their future destiny as members of the Communist society. The experiment consisted of taking infants away from their families and bringing them up in special centers, with the intention of preventing strong attachments to the parents, thus furthering the development of intensive group ties instead. Reich embraced this idea enthusiastically because, according to his theoretical model, he expected that the rearing of children without families would prevent the development of the Oedipus complex, with its concomitant defenses and inhibitions against free sexual expression and perfect genital gratification. He hailed the Russian undertaking as a means of abolishing neuroses in future generations.

In one of the meetings (I do not remember the date, but it was probably in 1929 or 1930), Reich presented these ideas in a very forceful, slightly provocative way. Freud listened attentively to Reich's presentation, then he said:

> It is not possible to discuss the subject seriously; it is much too difficult. But Reich's presentation has a weak point: it is dictated too much by therapeutic ambition. Therapeutic ambition is only halfway useful for science, for it is too tendentious. Free investigation is tremendously hampered by it. Therapeutic ambition leads to a kind of pragmatism, as in America, where everything is judged by its dollar value. As a scientific investigator, one should not take therapy into consideration. I said everything about it once in an earlier essay. [Freud was referring to his paper " 'Civilized' Sexual Morality and Modern Nervous Illness," published in 1908.] There I expressed the sharpest criticism of our sexual morality. But all suggestions of reforming the situation fail. One can do little more than patch up things.
>
> There is a second point in Reich's presentation against which I have to raise objections. He claims that if, in Russia, marriage and the family are abolished consistently, there will be no development of an Oedipus complex and, consequently, there will be no neuroses. This can be compared to treating a person's intestinal disorders by having him stop eating and at the same time putting a stopper into his anus. The family is, after all, based on a biological foundation. Besides, we have to say that the Oedipus complex is not the specific cause of neurosis. There is no single specific cause in the etiology of neurosis. Reich neglects the fact that there are many pregenital drive components that cannot possibly be discharged, even through the most perfect orgasm.
>
> Reich believes that a radical change in the child's social set-up would do away with mass neurosis. Nobody knows whether this is at all possible. However, theoretically it is most improbable. Besides, Reich's proposals are completely unpsychological. Economic changes [in the

Marxist sense] without psychology will not suffice. One also must always consider the influence of the past. [Here Freud was probably referring to the influence of tradition on the formation of the superego.]

Freud concluded his discussion with the following words: "It is impossible at present to say anything about the significance of the Russian experiment. Nobody can say anything about it before these children are thirty years old. I therefore suggest that we continue the discussion in thirty years" (at which time Freud would have been one hundred and four years old).

I remember one more sentence that I think Freud said in this meeting: "The only person who can radically abolish neurosis is Dr. Eisenbart." Dr. Eisenbart is a legendary figure in a children's song. He is an obnoxious braggart who betrays himself as a "con man" in the first stanza:

> Ich bin der Doktor Eisenbart
> Kurier die Leut' auf meine Art
> Ich mache dass die Blinden gehn
> Und dass die Lahmen wieder sehn.

> ("I am the Dr. Eisenbart
> And cure the people by my own method.
> I make the blind ones walk
> And the lame ones see again.")

Wilhelm Reich was visibly disappointed in Freud's reaction. His further development showed that he did not take Freud's "no" for an answer.

I remember that at another meeting Reich propagated his ideas in the discussion in a stubbornly persistent fashion. This was the only time that I ever saw Freud deliberately take on an authoritarian attitude. When Reich wanted to talk again after Freud had twice refuted his argument, Freud said very sternly: "He who wants to have the floor again and again shows that he wants to be right at all costs. I will not let you talk any more."

It is my impression that the disapproval Reich's theories met with, not only from Freud but also from most of the members of the psychoanalytic group in Vienna, pushed Reich even further along the path of becoming a pseudo-scientific-political activist. I will always feel that his deviation was a real loss to our science.

On 20 March 1930, the topic of the meeting was Freud's *Civilization and Its Discontents.* * I do not remember who reviewed the book. Freud spoke right after the reviewer had finished, which was unusual, and expressed a very critical attitude toward his own work. He called the structure of the book dilettantish because a narrow superstructure had been erected upon an unusually broad and diffuse foundation. He compared his book with the Tropaeum of Adamklissi. This Tropaeum was erected in the year 107 A.D. by the Roman emperor Trajan, near the Black Sea in present-day Romania. It commemorated Trajan's victories over the Dacians. Trajan's Tropaeum was the largest and most famous victory monument in antiquity. All that is left of it today is a big mound of stones and fragments of marble statuary and architecture. However, the reconstructions by archeologists show us that it had a very large and rustic foundation, one hundred fifty feet in diameter, on top of which stood a comparatively small architectural structure, extremely elaborate and adorned with an incredible richness of marble statuary commemorating the emperor's accomplishments on the battlefield. Freud's thorough humanistic education made it always easy for him to dip into his knowledge of the ancient past for examples and illuminating analogies, and he loved to do so.

After comparing his work to this Tropaeum, Freud explained the analogy. He said:

> The book does not deal exhaustively enough with the subject [namely, the discomfort in our culture], and on top of this rough foundation is put an overdifficult and overcompensating examination of the analytic theory of the feeling of guilt. But one does not make such compositions, they make themselves, and if one resists writing them down as

---

*I have always found the translation of the German title "Das Unbehagen in der Kultur" unsatisfactory. *Unbehagen* means "not feeling comfortable," referring to a psychic state; it means being disturbed by a feeling of insecurity or the state of insufficient gratification of basic needs. "Discomfort," in my opinion, comes nearer to *Unbehagen* than "discontent," which in German would be *Unzufriedenheit.* "Civilization" is not quite congruent with the German *Kultur;* however, "culture," the only other term in English at our disposal, has a slightly different meaning. I would translate the title as "Discomfort in our Culture."

thcy come, one does not know what the result will be. The analytic insight into the feeling of guilt was supposed to be in a dominant position.

The second reproach that Freud expressed toward his own work was that it showed a very significant defect.

> None of you has noted one omission in the work, and this is a gigantic disgrace. I myself noticed it only after the book was already printed. My omission is excusable, but not yours. I had good reason to forget something that I know very distinctly. If I had not forgotten it, but had written it down, it would have been unbearable. Thus, it was an opportunistic tendency that expressed itself through this forgetting. The forgotten piece belongs to the possibilities of happiness; in fact, this is the most important possibility because it is the only one that is psychologically unassailable. Thus, the book does not mention the only condition for happiness that is really sufficient.

And then Freud quoted two lines from an ode by Horace:

Si fractus inlabatur orbis
impavidum ferient ruinae.

He even translated the lines, which was unusual, since he assumed that we knew enough Latin to understand such quotations.

> If the firmament should break to pieces over him,
> the fragments will bury a fearless man.

(I will comment on this quotation later.)

Freud continued: "This possibility of happiness is so very sad. It is the person who relies completely upon himself. A caricature of this type is Falstaff. We can tolerate him as a caricature, but otherwise he is unbearable. This is the absolute narcissist. This unassailability by anything is given only to the absolute narcissist. My omission is a real defect in the presentation."

When I later looked up the Latin lines Freud had quoted—they come from the beginning of the third ode of Horace—I recognized that Freud had taken them out of context, perhaps because they were the only ones he remembered. He definitely misinterpreted their meaning. The stanzas that precede the two lines read as follows (in an English translation):

> He that is just, and firm in will
> Doth not before the fury quake
> Of mobs that instigate to ill
> Nor hath the tyrant's menace skill
> His fixed resolve to shake;
>
> Nor Auster, at whose wild command
> The Adriatic billows dash,
> Nor Jove's dread thunder-launching hand.

And then come the two verses:

> Yea, if the globe should fall, he'll stand
> Fearless amidst the crash.

The lines preceding the ones that Freud quoted, as well as the following ones, tell us that the brave man obtains his fearlessness and his emotional fortitude not from narcissism but from the strength of his moral convictions. It is the unwavering belief in his values that makes him so fearless. As I pointed out before, it was the possibility of being free to express ideas spontaneously and among friends which permitted Freud to speak with relative unconcern about the correctness of his remarks.

I no longer remember how it came about in this meeting that Freud later defended himself against the frequently expressed reproach (not made by any of the members present) that he did damage to people with his uncovering method. He said, with considerable emotional emphasis:

> During my whole life I have endeavored to uncover truths. I had no other intention and everything else was completely a matter of indifference to me. My single motive was the love of truth. It does no harm to anybody. You can unconcernedly tell people the worst. If we were told that a comet will destroy our planet in one hundred fifty years, nobody would let this announcement disturb him from enjoying his breakfast. The death of each of you is certain, mine obviously in a shorter time, and you do not let yourself be disturbed by this. Seven years ago I was told that I would have a maximum of five years to live, and since I took it

115

rather well, I can also tell mankind the most unpleasant things; it does not touch them.

At about this point Freud made the remark: "Actually, the truth is that we do not have so much culture that we could really feel uncomfortable in it." Then he went on:

My book is the outcome of the insight that our theory of instincts was insufficient. It has been said that I am trying to force the death instinct upon analysts. However, I am only like an old farmer who plants fruit trees, or like someone who has to go out of the house and leaves a toy behind so that the children will have something to play with while he is absent. I wrote the book with purely analytic intentions, based on my former existence as an analytic writer, in brooding contemplation, concerned to promote the concept of the feeling of guilt to its very end. The feeling of guilt is created by the renunciation of aggression. Now it's up to you to play with this idea. But I consider this the most important progress in analysis.

In this meeting Freud came to speak of Otto Rank. Freud had just been reading Rank's new book, and he objected to the *Seelenglauben* (belief in a soul) that was expressed in it. He said:

Rank was a highly gifted person, the most able and gifted of all the people. He then entered a second phase as a con man, in which he was driven only by the motivation to contradict Freud. Thus, he brings a new explanation of Hamlet as the son who no longer wants to be told anything by his father, and who therefore refuses to take on the son's obligation to avenge the father. This interpretation is *die groesste Lumperei*. [I cannot find a good translation for the word *Lumperei*. It is something a *Lump*—a scoundrel—would do or produce. I think "low type of fraudulence" comes close to *Lumperei*.] Hamlet is supposed to be the son who does not believe the father anymore. In his arguments, Rank puts himself on a very high horse and looks down on psychoanalysis. He uses the theory of relativity, the quantum theory, and the principle of indeterminism to express doubts about psychic causality, so that there is nothing left except soul and free will But psychoanalysis cannot possibly be an illusion [here Freud was obviously referring to the principle of determinism in our science]. The new discoveries might be bewildering to physicists, but psychology has always suf-

fered when the standpoints of other sciences are applied to
it.

And Freud closed his discussion by saying with strong emotional emphasis: "Leave psychology finally in peace; leave psychology to the psychologists."

And now I come to a story involving myself. It was in January 1931, when I was still rather young, that I had the audacity to
present a paper at one of the Wednesday meetings in the Berggasse. I chose a theoretical subject, "Zur Problematik der Sublim-
ierungslehre" (On the problem of the theory of sublimation).
The paper appeared in *Internationale Zeitschrift fuer Psychoanalyse* in 1930. (It has not been published in English.) It dealt with
the conceptual difficulty that arises when one compares some of
the statements in Freud's writings concerning sublimation. On
the one hand, Freud said repeatedly and in different papers that
repression precludes the sublimation of instinctual strivings; on
the other hand, he pointed out in "Three Essays on the Theory of
Sexuality" (1905) that one of the pathways of sublimation is reaction formation. Reaction formation, however, implies the repression of the drive against which the reactive dam is established. I
proposed a solution to this dilemma by suggesting that we might
have to distinguish between two forms of reaction formation: one
form identical to the countercathexis against strong unconscious
drive impulses, and another form in which the drive energy is
absorbed through the establishment of the reaction formation
itself. The compulsive countercathectic cleanliness established
against a strong unconscious drive toward anal messiness, in contrast to the normal cleanliness without a backlog of such pressing
anal needs, demonstrates the difference between the two types of
reaction formation.

I proposed that the theoretical problem—preclusion of sublimation by repression versus reaction formation as pathway of
sublimation—can be solved with the help of the concept of the
freely mobile cathexis energy without specific drive quality that
Freud established in *The Ego and the Id*. This energy is available
to the ego for its different tasks. If the process of sublimation,
which Freud equates with deinstinctualization, removes the
energy far enough from the original drive goal, it results in the

transformation of the drive energy into what Heinz Hartmann many years later called "neutralized energy." In my presentation I also established a scale of sublimatory results according to the distance from the original drive goal. On the near end of the continuum I placed the primitive ritual of the making of fire, of which it would be difficult to say whether it is a sexualized ego activity or a primordial sublimation of the libidinal drive. On the far end one would find the freely movable cathexis energy resulting from complete desexualization of drive energy. I proposed that the ego's strength depends on the amount of such *qualitaetslose* energy, that is, energy without specific drive quality that is at the disposal of the ego for its different tasks.

The discussion that followed my paper was very lively and, in general, in agreement with my thesis. Robert Waelder, in particular, somewhat aggressively pointed out that the contradiction that I had tried to reconcile in my paper actually existed in Freud's writings. He asked Freud point blank whether he considered sublimation as belonging to a category of concepts different from the other three instinctual vicissitudes, namely, reversal into its opposite, turning around against the subject, and repression. Freud had to agree, though a bit reluctantly, that sublimation does not quite belong in the same category as the other instinctual vicissitudes, although he had listed them together as *the* four instinctual vicissitudes in his first metapsychological paper. My pointing out the contradiction and the strong emphasis by Waelder and others made Freud slightly irritated, although during the coffee break he told Federn that he thought that it was a good paper, which Federn reported to me afterward.

After the intermission, Freud began the discussion by telling us how it came about that he developed the concept of sublimation. He had read in Heine's "Harzreise" about a young man who, out of juvenile sadistic mischief, cut the tail off of every dog he could get hold of, to the great indignation of the population in the Harz Mountains. This same person later became a surgeon, the famous Johann Friedrich Dieffenbach (1795-1847). Freud said:

> There someone does the same thing during his whole lifetime, first out of sadistic mischief and later to the benefit of mankind. I thought one could appropriately call this

change of significance of an action "sublimation." The concept of sublimation was immediately accepted, even by the enemies of psychoanalysis. People say: "This Freud is an abominable person; however, he has one rope with the help of which he can pull himself out of the sewer in which he dwells, and that is the concept of sublimation."

Next Freud talked about the formation of scientific concepts in general, laying stress on their preliminary nature. He emphasized that the attempt to form scientific concepts has to be very tentative and that it is not feasible to demand exactitude right away. Freud was obviously defending himself against what he must have felt as criticism of the contradiction in his theory of sublimation. He did not take notice of the fact that my paper was more concerned with the solution of the contradiction between some of the statements in his writings, which I tried to bring about with the help of Freud's concept of the freely mobile cathexis energy without drive quality of the ego. Freud spoke as if I had demanded a sharper delineation of what he considered preliminary concepts. In this context he said something that made a deep impression on me: "There exists something that one could call scientific tact." And at the end of his rather lengthy discourse he addressed me directly when he said: "This is a sermon of old age to you."

I would like to add to my report on these special meetings some comments by Freud which stuck in my mind although I do not remember the context in which he made them. One of them was: "The best attitude of the analytic patient is a benevolent skepticism." Another time, in a discussion about Alfred Adler, he remarked: "Adler took a bone out of psychoanalysis and now he sits over it in a corner and growls." When once the discussion in a meeting turned to the question of what means we have at our disposal to motivate a patient to undergo analysis, Freud pointed out that we promise him relief from his symptoms, an increase in his working capacity, and an improvement of his personal and social relationships. Anna Freud objected: "How can we do this when we are not sure that we can keep these promises?" Freud quickly answered: "There one can see that you are not a physician."

Freud once discussed the influence of outside events that

may have an effect on the therapeutic result. For example, he told us about a female patient of his who was convinced that an amulet that she wore on a necklace protected her family from harm. In therapy, Freud was able to show her the irrationality of this belief in the magical power of this amulet. With his encouragement the patient threw it into the Donau Canal, whereupon a dear relative of hers died suddenly. "Und das war das Ende der Behandlung," I remember Freud saying ("this was the end of the therapy").

Freud once said: "I am against lay analysts, whether they are physicians or not" (referring to the meaning of "lay" as "not initiated" or "not trained"). Another time he said: "Methodologists remind me of people who clean their glasses so thoroughly that they never have time to look through them." And once he remarked: "One of the great writers—there are only four or five—" and then he quoted Shakespeare or Goethe.

Once Freud remarked: "Schlagworte sind eine Denkersparnis" (slogans save the expenditure of thinking).

At this point I might as well quote another remark of Freud's that I had learned about but did not hear myself. It was reported to Freud that Wilhelm Stekel had once remarked that the dwarf standing on the head of the giant might see a little more than the giant himself. Stekel meant that he, although only a dwarf, stood on the head of the giant Freud. To this Freud quickly retorted: "Yes, but the louse in the astronomer's hair does not see a thing."

Freud once said, in one of these special meetings: "He who wants to be original as a psychoanalyst should not have read Nietzsche." Indeed, many of Freud's psychological findings had been expressed in an *aperçu* form in Nietzsche's writings. Freud's attention was repeatedly directed to instances where Nietzsche had already said something similar; he avoided reading Nietzsche in order to remain independent in his thinking. For Freud's seventieth birthday, Otto Rank gave him a luxury edition of Nietzsche's works. I do not know whether Freud read Nietzsche then.

Freud's theory of neuroses is based on the conflict between the libidinous and aggressive drives or between drive and antidrive structures in the mind, and he conceived of the drive as a mental representation of a biological need demanding gratification. He therefore expected that someday someone would find the psychochemical agents that are the basis of the drives. During the 1920s, the study of hormones dominated the biochemical field. The discovery of sex hormones increased the expectation that neuroses would be cured with the help of sex hormones, since the neuroses were based on sexual conflict. Two physicians gained notoriety on account of their attempts at sex hormone therapy for mental illness: the Viennese Eugen Steinach and the émigré Russian Serge Voronoff. Freud, who gave some weight to the possibility of hormonal treatment, became apprehensive that hormone therapy would be used indiscriminately. It was at one of the meetings, when hormone therapy was the subject of discussion, that he told us to do as much truly psychoanalytic research on neurotic patients as we could because he feared that our time might be limited.

At one of the meetings Freud asked us to do as much psychoanalytic research as we could because he feared that the time to do so was limited. He said: "I feel like an active explorer who knows that in a short time the ice will be closing in and the arctic winter will make any further exploration impossible. I feel like a wanderer in the fog who hears steps behind him coming nearer and nearer. Will he reach his goal before he is overwhelmed by the hostile follower?"

Freud compared the "hormone men with the syringe" with a blind giant in a china shop, and the psychological researcher to a sighted dwarf. The dwarf might be able to guide the blind giant so that he did not do too much damage. Freud's apprehension about the hormone therapy proved unfounded; the treatment proved ineffective and was soon abandoned. It was replaced by shock therapy, which in turn was followed by drug therapy, which still dominates the field. When used indiscriminately, drug therapy can still be compared to Freud's blind giant, although it is much more harmless than Freud expected hormone therapy would be.

Once, during my appointment as librarian of the Vienna Psychoanalytic Society, Freud wanted me to come to his study to accept some books that he wanted to give to the library. I appeared at the appointed time and was taken to his study. The maid, Paula, brought a laundry basket and Freud went through the rows of his books and selected particular volumes, which he gave to me to put into the basket. Out of one of the books fell a sheet of paper. I picked it up and saw that it was the announcement of the opening of Freud's office at Berggasse 19. I asked the professor if I could keep it. He said, "Of course, keep it." I walked home happy over the treasure I had acquired serendipitously. The announcement hangs framed in my studio. It reads:

> Docent Dr. Sigm. Freud
> beehrt sich anzuzeigen, dass er von Mitte September 1891 an
> > IX. Berggasse 19,
> wohnen und daselbst von 5-7 Uhr (auch 8-9 Uhr Frueh) ordinieren wird.
> > Wien, Datum des Poststempels

> (Docent Dr. Sigm. Freud
> has the honor to announce that, from the middle of September 1891, he will live at
> > 9 Berggasse 19,
> and will have office hours there from 5 to 7 P.M. [also 8-9 A.M.].
> > Vienna, Date of Postmark)

Some of Sigmund Freud's patients occasionally provided me with information on Freud's attitude as a therapist. John Dorsey told me that what impressed him most in Freud's attitude as an analyst was that he was completely natural. Philip Sarasin emphasized that he felt that Freud was continuously with him and that this supportive presence made it possible to go through all the emotional upheavals to which the analytic process exposes a patient. His remark fortified me in my conviction that the "blank screen" attitude of the analyst was not what Freud considered the optimal position. Sarasin's description of Freud's supportive way of dealing with the analysand led me to compare the attitude of the analyst with that of Virgil in Dante's *Divine Comedy*. There is a close parallel between Dante's wandering through hell under the mentorship of Virgil and the analytic situation and treatment process. Virgil starts his role as mentor-companion at the entrance to the inferno. There, Dante is puzzled by the famous inscription "per me si va nella città dolente . . ." (through me lies the road to the city of grief . . .). After having read the inscription, Dante turns to Virgil with the question: "Maestro, il senso lor' m'e duro" (Maestro, it is hard for me to get the meaning), and promptly receives his first information. The analyst's role is similar to Virgil's, leading and explaining the amazing perceptions in the nether world, there of the inferno, here of the unconscious. In my opinion, the analyst's attitude should be the same as Virgil's: from the very beginning continuously accompanying, comforting, fortifying, explaining, and encouraging. The analyst has to share with Virgil another feature. Like Virgil, he must be unshaken by the horrors of the Acheron. It is the analyst's ability to face the dangers of the unconscious as well as the bewilderment by the primary process which enables him to go along continuously and actively with the thought processes of the analysand. It gives the patient the feeling of being protected by the holding presence of the analyst.

Freud did not hestitate to transcend the so-called classical or orthodox behavior of the analyst as it was prescribed by training institutes. He freely deviated from the straight and narrow path of "impersonality" and indulged in "parameters" that would have met with an outcry of indignation by the adherents to a strict and "sterile" attitude of the analyst which is supposed to present *the* classical model of the analyst's behavior. Editha and I were once invited for dinner by an American psychiatrist who had just started her analysis with Freud. She had come to Vienna with her husband, also a physician, who wanted to improve his knowledge and skill in his specialty at the Vienna school of medicine. The woman told us that in one of the first sessions with Freud she remarked that her husband had not found any cigars that suited him in the Vienna tobacco shops. (Tobacco was a monopoly in Austria and the *Tabak-Trafik* could sell only *Regie* products that were made in government-owned tobacco factories.) When the patient reported her husband's complaint, Freud got up from his chair and walked into his adjacent study. He returned with a handful of cigars, which he gave to the patient for her husband. He also told her the address of the shop on the Kohlmarkt where these imported cigars could be bought. She said that her husband was very satisfied with the brand and had already bought a whole box at the specialty shop. This vignette of Freud's behavior as a therapist shows the flexibility of his attitude vis-à-vis the patient.

However, one always has to keep in mind the famous Latin proverb: "Quod licet Jovi non licet bovi," meaning "What is permitted to Jove is not permitted to an ordinary ox."

On the occasion of postwar visits to Vienna, I had lunch several times with the famous "Wolfman." He too emphasized how free and easy-going Freud was in the analytic situation and that Freud and he not infrequently talked about subjects other than his analytic material. It is certain that Freud did not suffer from the parameter phobia that became rampant among analysts in the fifties and sixties. Fortunately, at present the "blank screen" prescription for the analyst has been replaced by a more relaxed attitude.

It has often been mentioned that Freud was particularly fond of children. On one occasion, Editha took our oldest daughter, who was then three years old, to meet Anna Freud, who, naturally, was interested in the children of her coworkers. The Freuds had rented a villa for the summer in the western outskirts of Vienna. Anna Freud met my wife and daughter in the garden; and the professor happened to step out, accompanied by his dog. While Anna Freud talked to Editha, my daughter asked Freud: "Wie heisst Dein Hund?" (What's the name of your dog?), using *Du*, a form of familiarity in German. She had not yet learned to use the respectful *Sie*. The professor told her the dog's name and lovingly stroked her blond hair. Then he gave her a pear, for which she thanked him politely. It was a brief encounter, but she later spoke repeatedly of the old gentleman who had been so nice to her. Editha also was very much impressed by the kindness with which Freud had spoken to our child.

I believe it was during the meeting in which Theodor Reik had reviewed Freud's book *The Future of an Illusion* that Freud said: "I have just received a letter from an American physician which I would like to read to you." With this he got up from his chair and went to his study to fetch the letter. He read it to us in the original English. The letter reported on the religious conversion that the writer of the letter had experienced when he was still a medical student. He said that the sweet face of an old woman to be dissected made him think that there is no God, for God would not permit such an outrage. But after a short period of denial he received undeniable proof of the existence of God and of the truth in the Bible. Freud gave us a psychoanalytic explanation of the dynamics of this conversion. I had the impression that the explanation occurred to him on the spot while he talked to us and was not in any way premeditated or prepared. Editha, who had also been present at the meeting, had the same impression. We truly observed his great mind at work.

Two days later, the manuscript of Freud's paper "Ein religioeses Erlebnis" (A religious experience)* was delivered to the psychoanalytic publishing house where Editha worked as editor. The manuscript repeated almost verbatim what Freud had told us in the meeting.

What I have reported here is only a fraction of the content of these special meetings at Berggasse 19. They took place around fifty years ago, but the atmosphere and spirit is still vividly present in me. They were the highlights of my psychoanalytic living.

I saw Freud's wife, whom one addressed as "Frau Professor" a few times very fleetingly at Berggasse 19, though I never spoke to her. I was introduced to her at Freud's seventieth birthday and I kissed her hand, as was customary. She impressed me as a very refined elderly lady. Her face was pale, but it expressed kindness and dignified reserve. Her demeanor evoked respect. My contacts were too fleeting to be able to say more about "Frau Professor."

Standard Edition, vol. 21, p. 169.

VI. Remarks on Some Personalities

In this chapter I shall present portraits of my colleagues as I came to know them through personal contact and as I observed them in meetings and at social gatherings. I will also relate some of the stories I heard from others, but only when they contribute to the characterization of a personality and highlight features that I myself observed. I will designate "hearsay" stories as such and relate them only if I consider the source of the information reliable.

The analysts in Vienna during this period fall into three groups. The first group consists of the older members of the Vienna Psychoanalytic Society before World War I. To the second group belong those members who joined the movement after 1918 but before the establishment of the institute. The third group is made up of members who joined the society after they attended the regular training course at the institute. I will discuss the personalities in each category as they occur to me. Naturally, the importance of their roles in the society and to me personally influences the order of my description.

MEMBERS OF THE VIENNA PSYCHOANALYTIC SOCIETY BEFORE WORLD WAR I

I speak of Dr. Paul Federn first because he was such an impressive personality. His character is difficult to describe, since it consisted of marked contradictions. For most of the period with which I am concerned in this report he was vice-president of the society and chaired the society meetings, since Freud, the president, could not attend. This gave me plenty of opportunity to observe him in action. He was a man of great intensity and he was deeply devoted to the cause of psychoanalysis. I respected him for his sincerity, his openness of expression, and his ardent fervor to be just, often against his own emotional inclination. At times one could sense an effort to do what his strict conscience considered right, and one could feel his struggle against an inclination to temperamental, spontaneous reactions. He fought noticeably and victoriously within himself for self-control and for what he considered right.

As a clinician, Federn was an unusually keen observer of what he termed "ego feelings." He devoted himself to the minute studies of "ego boundaries"; his unusual sensitivity to ego states enabled him to observe in himself and in others the subtle changes of the extension and of the intensity of cathexis of the ego boundaries. He attempted to explain theoretically the observed ego phenomena with the help of the concept of the cathexis with libido or aggressive energy. Federn had great difficulty expressing his theoretical conception with the spoken and the written word. Therefore, his papers are hard to understand. This might be why his scientific work found relatively little recognition. For most people, myself among them, it was difficult to follow him. I tried very hard to understand him, because I felt that Federn, with his keen observation and his highly sensitive empathy with patients, was attempting to contribute something of real importance to metapsychology. I had the impression that Freud did not go along with Federn's ideas. Freud never referred to Federn's series of studies of ego states in his writings, a fact that must have hurt Federn very deeply, since Federn was a loyal and most devoted follower of Freud.

Paul Federn was also a stimulating and inspiring teacher. I received one of my finest learning experiences as a trainee in a seminar that Federn conducted on Freud's "Interpretation of Dreams." Federn taught us to read this most important of Freud's works with great care, literally sentence by sentence. His comments on each sentence made us aware of the richness of the connections between Freud's own dream associations, the wealth of his ideas, the depth of meaning in every one of Freud's statements, and the revolutionary impact of the body of Freud's work.

127

I remember Federn saying to us: "There is only one other book that is read and has been read with such care and diligence as one should devote to reading Freud's dream book, that is the Bible." Federn made great efforts to increase the public's awareness of the new science. Together with his friend Heinrich Meng, he published the psychoanalytic *Volksbuch,* in which the authors tried to make psychoanalytic knowledge accessible to the general public.

Federn's physical appearance was impressive. A black beard framed his face, his brows were black and bushy, and his high forehead extended into the bald top of his head. His gestures were alive and intense and often vividly expressed his struggle to find the appropriate verbal expression. He had the habit of raising one arm while bending his head to the side in his strenuous effort to give birth to exact words for his ideas. Among the analytic group, his frequent slips of the tongue and other parapraxes were famous. Once after he gave a lengthy explanation of his ideas, Federn closed with a question directed to the group. He asked: "Did I understand myself?" He obviously had wanted to ask: "Did I make myself understood?" His slip of the tongue betrayed his awareness of a certain lack of clarity in his own thinking.

It is my impression that Federn's frequent slips of the tongue betrayed a deep-seated ambivalence that sometimes found expression also in his actions. He was always very friendly to me and observed my analytic growth with benevolence and support. One day when I was still in the beginning of my analytic practice, he said to me: "Sterba, I had a very well paying and excellent case for you, but I have sent him to someone else." Knowing Federn, I took no offense at this. His deeply sincere intentions and the honesty of his personal and scientific struggle with himself demanded my respect and admiration.

The Federns always spent their summer vacation in Goisern, an alpine village in the Salzkammergut. Goisern was not far from Gmunden, on Lake Traunsee, where we spent our vacations at Editha's family home. Each summer vacation, I rode my bicycle to Goisern to visit with the Federns. The route led along Lake Traunsee and through Traun Valley, a most beautiful alpine landscape. It was a highlight of my vacation which I enjoyed for many years, and I looked forward to the wild strawberries that

Mrs. Federn always served with fresh milk. Most of the time the Hungarian analyst István Hollos was in Goisern as a houseguest of the Federns. I esteemed Hollos for his friendly attitude and his highly cultured personality.

Between our wide-ranging discussions about professional and cultural subjects, we played table tennis; Federn was very good at it and regularly beat me. Once Federn visited us in Gmunden and we took a swim in Lake Traunsee. I made a movie of Federn as he slowly went into the water, but he forbade me ever to show it to anybody, and I never did.

I would like to quote one remark that Federn made to me in the late spring of 1933, shortly after Hitler had come to power in Germany. On our walk home from a society meeting, we were discussing Germany's newly established Nazi regime. Federn said about the new German rulers: "I give them twelve years." And it was exactly twelve years later that the "Third Reich of a Thousand Years" collapsed.

After our flight from Vienna, we met Paul Federn in Paris at the International Congress of Psychoanalysis in 1938. We were refugees burdened by the uncertainty of our future. Federn was visibly depressed and said to me with a sigh: "There are too many people in the boat," referring to the many family members he would have to support with his future earnings. However, he settled in New York and I think his financial situation there was satisfactory until his health failed.

My last contact with Federn was an exchange of letters. A few months before his death, he sent me the typed manuscript of a paper whose author was not mentioned. In a letter accompanying the manuscript Federn wrote that he was deeply hurt because I had not quoted his work in the paper. I returned the manuscript to him with the assurance that I would certainly have quoted him if I had been the author, but I was not. He answered me, excusing himself for the mistake, and added that he had hoped that he had finally overcome his inclination for such slip actions. Soon afterward I learned that he had committed suicide to avoid a long, agonizing death from the cancer with which he was afflicted. The memory of this outstanding personality is highly honored in my heart.

A quite different personality was Eduard Hitschmann.

Although he and Federn had worked together in internal medicine at the same *Klinik* (university hospital), there was considerable antagonism between the two personalities. Federn often seemed irritated by Hitschmann's mere presence. I think what Federn objected to in Hitschmann was the latter's biting wit. It may be best to illustrate Hitschmann's sarcastic humor by some examples. He once said to me: "The best *Faelle* [cases] for psychoanalysis were the *Felle* [furs or pelts] of the old Eitingon." In German the pronunciation of both words *Faelle* and *Felle* is identical. From what I heard, Max Eitingon's father had been a fur merchant in Leipzig and had accumulated a considerable fortune that enabled Max Eitingon to make a vital financial contribution to the establishment of the Berlin Psychoanalytic Institute. Hitschmann's remark was an excellent pun in German, but, like most puns, it is untranslatable. Another example: at approximately the time when Ferenczi reached his sixtieth birthday, he published his book *Thalassa.* The German title of the book is *Versuch einer Genitaltheorie* (Attempt at a theory of genitality). According to the story, in a toast that Hitschmann made at a celebration for Ferenczi's birthday, he made the somewhat tactless but witty remark: "Now that Ferenczi has reached his sixtieth year, he writes on the theory of genitality." Hitschmann emphasized the word *theory.*

When Anna Freud took over the chair of the society meetings in the late thirties, Hitschmann remarked to me, pointing at the chair, "There Freud had been sitting and taught us the *drives,* and now Anna sits there and teaches us the *defenses,*" referring to Anna's somewhat ascetic and distancing personality.

On the other hand, Hitschmann was a very significant contributor to our science, particularly in the beginning of the analytic movement. He had a great literary interest and knowledge. One of his best papers was a fictional treatise titled: "Goethe ueber die Psychoanalyse" (Goethe on psychoanalysis). In this article Hitschmann quoted many sentences out of Goethe's works and arranged them in such a skillful way that they appeared to affirm psychoanalysis. He presented it as if psychoanalysis was a discovery at Goethe's time. Hitschmann imitated Goethe's style most skillfully, particularly as it appears in Goethe's famous conversations with Eckermann. Unfortunately, even the best translation would not do justice to the superb imitation of the way in which in Hitschmann's article Goethe was supposed to express himself to Eckermann concerning psychoanalysis. I consider it a masterpiece of analytic-literary fiction. Hitschmann's scientific field was the libido theory; he was particularly interested in disturbances of the adult sexual function: male impotence and female frigidity. He did not fully participate in the development of ego psychology. The prime time period of his work was the libido-dominated phase of psychoanalysis. In 1911, he had already published an introduction to psychoanalysis which presented the first overview of the new science.

Hitschmann wrote a series of psychobiographical studies in which he tried to apply psychoanalytic understanding to the biographical data and their connection with the creations of the personalities of Gottfried Keller, Knut Hamsun, Selma Lagerloef, Max Dauthenday, Emanuel Swedenborg, Johannes Brahms, Franz Schubert, Franz Werfel, William James, Johann Eckermann, Samuel Johnson, and James Boswell.

Another field of Hitschmann's special interest was the analysis of dreams. I remember particularly some useful advice of his concerning the technique of dream analysis, which, however, one should not take too strictly. He illustrated it with a comparison. In doing dream analysis, he said, one should imagine that one writes down the elements of the manifest dream on a sheet of paper. Then one associates to each element, independent from the others, and writes down the associations on a second sheet. After having done this with all the manifest elements, one discards the first sheet. In this way one has extracted the latent dream thoughts and can more easily recognize their connections and the relations between them. One of the most deceiving features of the manifest dream is thus eliminated, namely, the logical or pseudological connections established between the manifest elements by the secondary elaboration. This is the best way to recognize the hidden meaning of the dream. I found Hitschmann's advice very useful in analyzing my own dreams, in analyzing the dreams of my patients, and in teaching dream interpretation.

Hermann Nunberg was highly respected by the analytic group. He was a small man whose appearance did not impress one right away. He was soft spoken and did not possess the verbal facility with which some of the other members were so richly endowed. But one always listened to the content of whatever he said, for it was always significant and based on a vast experience of careful observations. He was mild in his manner and had his aggressive drives well under control. However, I remember a slip of the tongue which he made in one of the Kinderseminars of the younger members, which took place in his bachelor apartment. The subject of the discussion was therapeutic results and failures. Nunberg wanted to say "If the treatment is unsuccessful," but instead he said, "If the mistreatment is successful," which would make one suspect that he might have been somewhat sadistic toward his patients. However, from several patients whom I treated after him, I know that Nunberg could be extremely warm, sympathetic, and not only analytically but also humanly helpful in emergency situations. I myself had an experience in which he showed his readiness to be of assistance and help.

As a very young analyst, I once turned to Nunberg for advice in a very difficult situation. A male patient of mine was the protégé of a lady of the highest aristocracy. The lady was obviously infatuated with him. He used his analysis for his different maneuvers (and for his own financial gain) in his relationship with the lady, not unlike a confidence man. This secondary gain from his analysis caused considerable difficulties in his therapy. One day, the lady appeared unannounced in my office and, since I had opened the door myself, I could not refuse to receive her. She was in great distress, since her protégé's behavior had made her doubt his sincerity. I was able to give her evasive answers without betraying anything that would have been damaging or embarrassing to my patient. When the lady left, she implored me not to tell my patient that she had come to see me, which the situation forced me to promise her. I was in a terrible dilemma, for in my training I had learned that one should never have any dealings with anybody in the patient's surroundings without the patient's consent or at least his knowledge. In my distress I called Hermann Nunberg for advice before I saw the patient the next morning. He invited me to come to him immediately. When I arrived at Nunberg's apartment he suggested that we take a walk together. It was a warm summer day and we took a stroll in the quiet area around the *Rathaus* (city hall). I told him my experience and how uncomfortable I felt about having promised the lady to keep her visit a secret from my patient. Nunberg reassured me that I had handled the situation correctly. He told me that as an analyst one has to keep such a meeting with a third person a secret if the communication would be of harm or embarrassment to anybody. There are circumstances in which an analyst has to make an exception to the rule of absolute candidness vis-à-vis the patient, and there is no need to feel bad about this. His comforting words soothed my professional conscience and I was very grateful. The analysis of the patient continued undisturbed by this incident. Since then I have encountered other situations that have brought me in conflict with the otherwise strict obligation to absolute candidness toward the patient, and Nunberg's advice has always served me as a useful guideline.

Nunberg was not the type to be interested or active in sports. However, since we younger members were great skiing enthusiasts, he wanted to try this activity. It happened that at that time Helene Deutsch had rented for the weekend a country house in Seebenstein, a village situated in a part of the Alps southwest of Vienna called the Wechsel, a well-known skiing area. She had invited some of us, including Nunberg, to visit her on a winter Sunday so that we could spend the day skiing on the hills surrounding her house. Because Nunberg was a beginner, we encouraged him to try to slide down a very gentle slope. Unfortunately, there was a tree in the middle of the slope. Nunberg seemed to be magnetically attracted by this tree, because, in spite of the advice we shouted at him, he landed in front of the tree on his back with both skis up in the air along the tree trunk. He was unhurt, but he was helplessly stuck, incapable of getting his skis back on the snow and struggling to get up like a turtle lying on its back. We had to take his skis off his boots and help him to get on his feet. He walked through the snow back to Helene Deutsch's house—and I think he never tried skiing again. However, being a sportsman did not really matter in our circle. Sports for us were a pleasure, not a field for competition, and not being good in sports did not diminish the value of a person if he excelled in matters of scholarship, culture, or art. Nunberg's great strength was his scholarship and vast clinical knowledge, to which his many publications are witness.

Ludwig Jekels, another of the older members, came originally from Warsaw and joined the society in 1910. He had translated Freud's writings into Polish. After World War I, he settled in Vienna. Jekels's vast experience as a therapist and his fruitful analytic thinking were highly regarded. His contributions in discussions were rare, but always of real significance. More than others, he was respected by Freud, and he had more personal contact with Freud than most of the older members. I was told that he became Freud's partner in the card game that was held regularly every Saturday night at Freud's. I had very little personal contact with Jekels, although he visited us once in our summer home in Gmunden and seemed to be impressed by the old family home of Editha's and the superb view from the balcony over Lake Traunsee with its frame of high mountain chains; he congratulated us on the wonderful place we called our own. Once when I took a walk with him in Vienna—we had so many opportunities for beautiful walks on the Ringstrasse—Jekels expressed a pessimistic outlook for psychoanalysis. "Someday," he said, "we will have to pay dearly for the high expectations that we have placed in the effectiveness of our therapy." He predicted that the public would feel deceived by our claim of the curative power of the analytic method. I did not know Ludwig Jekels well enough to know whether I should attribute this gloomy remark to a momentary depressive mood or to a general depressive attitude. However, I cannot remember that I ever saw him laughing. My youthful optimism and the positive therapeutic results that I had achieved with my patients prevented me from accepting his predictions.

This conversation took place many years before Freud published "Analysis, Terminable and Interminable." In the paper Freud discusses the limitations of the analytic therapy which our youthful optimism had led us to deny or to attribute to our own insufficiently developed technique. But Jekels's prediction has to a great extent come true, particularly in recent years. The promotion of drug therapy and different short-term treatment methods has discredited psychoanalysis in the public eye. However, my experience of many years as a psychoanalytic practitioner has increased my conviction that psychoanalysis, when used for the right cases, is superior to any other treatment method. Analysis is more than a symptomatic therapy. Analysis with a good therapist leads to self-insight, which enhances the growth of personality, widens the patient's world view and understanding of others, and increases true creativity. It cannot be replaced by any of the many short-cut therapies that are temporarily in vogue and follow each other in rapid succession. But I often think of Jekels's pessimistic prophecy when I contemplate the present low standing of psychoanalysis in the public eye.

August Aichhorn was the very opposite of Ludwig Jekels. He was of a somewhat stocky build, his round face sported a well-trimmed mustache and a goatee, and he had vivid, confidence-inspiring eyes, almost always with a twinkle in them. He reminded me of Frans Hals's joyful portraits of middle-aged Dutch burghers. One felt immediately at ease with him. His warmth and relaxed attitude invited instant trust. This quality was his great gift in dealing with some of the most difficult forms of psychopathology: waywardness, delinquency, and addiction. He knew how to gain the confidence of the most mistrusting youthful patients whom he took into treatment. He also gained their respect because he could always outsmart them. For the therapy of these difficult youths, it was of equal importance to inspire trust in the parent or parent substitute of the patient. I remember that he once said in a seminar how absolutely necessary it was to create a strong transference to the therapist and a strong belief in his therapeutic power in the mother of a rebellious boy when, for instance, the mother had to clean the door again and again after the boy repeatedly hurled an inkstand against it. What helped Aichhorn so much, particularly when he treated patients from the lower class, was that he spoke the typical Viennese dialect. He had a profound dislike of aggressive castrative mothers; he termed them "the women with the straight razor." I heard him say about such a mother who mistreated her children by her destructive attitude: "She belongs in the crematorium, but with no streetcar ticket; she will have to walk there!" The crematorium of Vienna was far in the outskirts, a good two hours' walk from the inner city.

In meetings, which he rarely attended, Aichhorn remained

silent except when he presented a paper. He obviously did not feel comfortable among the many "highbrow" intellectuals. He was not at home with the theoretical concepts of metapsychology. Besides, he had not had the same humanistic education that we had acquired; he was "only" a schoolteacher. It did not seem to give him any assurance that we all had the greatest respect for him. Even the fact that Freud himself had acknowledged Aichhorn as a pioneer in his field, someone who had opened new vistas of therapy, did not give him more self-assurance in the meetings. I still find it regrettable that we did not see and hear more of him, since he had so much to offer.

I remember Wilhelm Hoffer as a most pleasant colleague. During the twenties, he was busy studying medicine and could not be very active in the analytic society. After World War I, he and Siegfried Bernfeld had conducted a therapeutic home for refugee children in a suburb of Vienna, and his main interest was the observation of children. He was mild mannered, warm, and most pleasantly friendly. I was therefore surprised when he invited me once to attend a boxing match. This was the first and only time that I attended a fight. It was on a hot summer evening and the boxing ring was outside in a well-known large beergarden near Schoenbrunn. The ring was illuminated by brilliant floodlights and I can still see the sprays of sweat caused by a well-placed heavy punch in the face of one fighter. I found the spectacle unpleasantly brutal, but Hoffer enjoyed it with great enthusiasm. I had not expected that such open aggression would give him any pleasure. When he married Hedwig Schaxel, our contact with Willy was very much reduced, though our friendly feelings toward him remained unchanged.

Another of the older members was Dr. Alfred Winterstein. His full name was Alfred Freiherr von Winterstein. He was one of the few members belonging to the nobility. When someone in his house answered the telephone, they spoke of him as "Baron Freddy." He was indeed a noble character. At the meetings he was not very active in the discussions; however, in private conversations one learned to value his insight, his judgment, and his knowledge of history and literature. His great merit was that he, together with August Aichhorn, upheld the truncated remnants of psychoanalysis in Vienna over the seven years of Nazi rule.

Dr. Hermine von Hug-Hellmuth is known as the first psychoanalyst who tried psychoanalytic therapy with children. Her treatment method was analogous to that used for adult patients and the results were not promising. I do not remember having met her. Soon after I joined the analytic group, she was murdered by her nephew, whom she had brought up. I do not know any details of this tragic story. The nephew was sentenced to several years in prison. When he was released in the early thirties, he demanded financial support from the psychoanalytic society because he claimed to have been a victim of psychoanalytic treatment by his analyst-aunt. The nephew's request was denied and I never heard anything more about him.

Fritz Wittels played a peculiar role in the analytic community. He had been a participant in the earliest meetings of the society, which he joined in 1906 when it was still the Wednesday Society. Irritated by various criticisms against him, particularly by Carl Jung, he left the society in 1910 and tried to associate with Wilhelm Stekel. When Stekel separated from Freud, Stekel and Wittels published their own "psychoanalytic" journal. Their theories and technique, although derived from classical analysis, deviated from it in many essential points. In the midtwenties Wittels asked to be reinstated as a member of the Vienna Psychoanalytic Society. When Freud was asked what he thought about Wittels's wish to return to the society, he was in favor of accepting him. And so Wittels reappeared in the meetings. In the beginning he seemed to be somewhat unaware of the state of development of psychoanalysis at the time of his return. We all were flabbergasted when, in one of the first society meetings that Wittels attended, he declared that in his whole practice he had never seen any manifestation of a castration complex—certainly an amazing statement for a member of the psychoanalytic society! But Wittels was a very intelligent and clever person and he quickly adjusted to the scientific and practice level of the group. He was a prolific writer and his bibliography from the time of his reentry into the society is very impressive. He had published novels and a biography of Freud (1924). In the latter book he presented Freud as intolerant of any opinion that deviated from his own. The book contains a number of misconceptions concerning Freud's personality. In 1933, Wittels wrote a supplement to the biography which is essentially an apology for his mispresentation of Freud's personality. He corrected his misunderstandings about psychoanalytic theory and technique. In the midthirties, Wittels left Vienna for the United States.

MEMBERS WHO JOINED THE SOCIETY AFTER
WORLD WAR I

René Spitz became a member in 1925. According to what he told me when we were in exile in the United States, he had been in analysis with Sigmund Freud in 1910. Spitz gained his world-wide recognition after his immigration to the United States. Before that, for most of my professional years in Vienna, he lived and worked in Berlin and returned to Vienna only in 1933. His observations of the reactions of emotionally deprived infants and small children, made in the United States, and the theoretical conceptions based on his studies of children deprived of maternal care are of such importance that in my memory they have over-shadowed any recollection of his activity in the society of Vienna. I had the impression, during the short time I knew him in Vienna, that he was a kind of "gentleman-psychoanalyst," or something of a dabbler in the field. His later work, which helped to develop the object relations theory, certainly contradicted my earlier impression.

Robert Waelder came to the field of psychoanalysis from physics, in which he held a Ph.D. When Editha and I became acquainted with him, we were both impressed by the acuity of his mind, the vastness of his knowledge, and his ability to verbalize his thoughts in a masterly fashion. His facial expression conveyed in a peculiar way the intense oral pleasure he derived from the physical activity of speaking. Sometimes one had the feeling that he molded his words with his mouth. It was surprising that Waelder showed a certain unworldliness that stood in contrast to the vastness of his scientific and literary knowledge. I have no idea what his family background was, but many things that were self-evident to sophisticated people seemed foreign to him. During the time I knew him, he acquired the ways of our world very quickly. Most noticeable in the beginning was his lack of taste in the choice of his clothing, which was something grotesquely mismatched. I remember his wearing egg-yolk-colored shoes with a dark suit.

In the twenties, the group of younger analysts developed an enthusiasm for modern ballroom dancing—the Charleston, tango, and fox trot were in vogue at that time—and most of us, along with some of the older analysts, took dancing lessons. Robert Waelder participated eagerly in the efforts to learn these modern dances. However, his short and somewhat stout figure and the awkwardness of his movements made him a poor dancer; at the same time a certain exaggeration in his movements made him conspicuous on the dance floor. He told us once that he must have acquired some unusual mannerisms while dancing, for recently when he had danced in a nightclub, the other couples on the dance floor stopped dancing and the whole room looked at his, I assume, bizarre gyrations and broke out in loud laughter. His partner asked him to stop dancing because she felt embarrassed. It was with great naïveté that he related this incident to us, as if he were unaware of the ridiculous situation in which his mannerisms had placed him and his partner.

Another situation showed how much out of contact with the surroundings Waelder could be at times. In the spring of 1927 a dramatic political event took place in Vienna. Twelve members of the Social Democratic party—the party of the blue-collar workers and many progressively minded intellectuals—had been killed in a brawl by some Fascistic hotheads in Schattendorf, a village near Vienna. The killers were brought to court and the jury acquitted them. It was on a Friday morning that the news of this juridical injustice spread among the Viennese population. It enraged the working people, and great masses of them spontaneously left their place of work, assembled on the Ringstrasse (the famous avenue that circles the inner city), and marched to the Palace of Justice, where they stormed into the offices, poured gasoline on all the legal files that were accessible, and set them on fire. The fire spread quickly through most of the building, and the masses prevented the fire fighters from approaching. The police were quickly armed with rifles and ordered to shoot at the mob, which resulted in casualties. I was unaware of the uproar in the inner city and in the early afternoon I walked from our apartment in the sixth district on my usual route to the Herzstation to see my ambulatorium patients. Because of roadblocks set up by the police, I had to make some detours. On my way, I heard shooting, first in the distance, then quite close, and several times had to take cover in the entrance of a building. I was somewhat late in arriving at the Herzstation and I learned only from my first patient, who also arrived late, what had gone on in the inner city. Most of my patients that afternoon came late, and some did not come at all. Very few people had radios at that time; they learned the news from the newspaper or by word of mouth. The whole city was feverishly excited and enraged at the brutality of the police. As a protest to the aggressive action of the police, the unions declared a general strike.

The following day, Saturday, all public offices remained closed and all public transportation ceased. Editha and I stayed home and discussed the events with friends over the telephone, which was still working. A week earlier we had planned a get-together with Robert Waelder at our apartment for Saturday afternoon. Of course, we did not expect that he would keep the appointment, since he lived quite a distance from us and there was no public transportation functioning. The shortest route for Waelder to our apartment led through the inner city, which one could not enter because of the roadblocks. We had made ourselves quite comfortable, since we expected to spend a quiet evening at home, when around 7:00 P.M. the doorbell rang. I opened the door and there stood Robert Waelder, surprised at our appearance in housecoats. He asked us, most astonished, whether we had not expected him. We told him that we had not, because of the tumultuous events in the city. He had no idea what had gone on in the inner city and only when we showed him from our window the black smoke rising from the direction of the Palace of Justice did he realize why we had not expected him. He said that he had noticed that the police did not let anyone walk through the inner city, so he took a detour through the outer districts; it just took him an hour longer than it would have otherwise.

The burning of the Palace of Justice led to the establishment of the Heimwehr, a reactionary paramilitary organization like the Black Shirts in Italy. The Heimwehr was established to counter-act the Social Democrats, who then ruled by majority in the city of Vienna. The founding of the Heimwehr was the beginning in Austria of Fascism, which, supported by Mussolini, developed into the suppressive force to which the Austrian Socialist party succumbed a few years later. Eventually the Heimwehr gave way to Germany's National Socialism, with all its terror and the abolishment of all liberties.

However, on that memorable Saturday evening we were glad to be able to discuss the events with our friend, and I remember that Waelder had much to say about their ominous significance as the beginning of Fascism in Austria. Future political developments proved him right. The time we spent with Waelder was always profitable; his excellent logical mind, the vast areas of his knowledge, and his verbal expressiveness and quick wit made him an excellent *Gespraechspartner.* * Waelder's extensive knowledge and his vast vision are easily seen, particularly in his later writings. We enjoyed his company at every occasion; it was always a great pleasure to listen to somebody who is justifiably called a *gescheiter Mensch.*

Gescheit in German means more than "intelligent"; it means a person who can use his intelligence in a clever, farsighted manner, who has a superior insight into situations and relationships and a vast stock of knowledge in many areas. Freud once said in one of the meetings in the Berggasse: "It is of no harm if the analyst is a *gescheiter Mensch."*

The most brilliant example of a *gescheiter Mensch* was Freud himself. His store of knowledge was inexhaustible. Bernfeld told me that he once had lunch with Freud in a trattoria at the Villa Adriana, near Rome. He spoke with greatest admiration of what an incredible store of information Freud showed during their conversation. He not only spoke with the expertise of an archeologist about the different ruins in the vast area of Hadrian's summer residence, he also knew the different trees, plants, and

---

*The German *Gespraech* means more than conversation. The English *discourse* is somewhat too heavy to designate the easy give and take of the *Gespraech*, which, however, deserves the title only when it deals with subjects that transcend immediate personal interests and broadens out into issues of general significance. Goethe's *Gespraeche mit Eckermann* are the best paradigms. Goethe said "What is more valuable than gold? The light. What is more precious than light? The *Gespraech."* (I quote this from memory, and the quote might not be exact.)

flowers that grew around them, and he was even knowledgeable about the Frascati wine that they enjoyed together. Bernfeld found it amazing that one man should know so much about so many different areas. What made this possible was, first, that Freud had an almost photographic memory, and, second, that he was an extremely fast reader who could retain the content indelibly in his memory. Both Max Schur and Joseph Weinman told me that when Freud was reading a book, he did it so fast that it appeared as if he was slowly thumbing through it. To this ability was added an unusual facility to recall the information that he had once absorbed.

In 1926, we met Waelder by chance on the Lido in Venice. He was then still an analytic theoretician and worked for the Psychoanalytic Publishing House. In our talks with him we said how fascinating the analytic work was for us, to which he replied that it was inconceivable to him to sit hour after hour behind patients. I do not know when he changed his mind and what made him change it; I only know that later he practiced analysis and he acquired the reputation of being an outstanding analytic therapist and supervisor. Our friendship with Robert Waelder was a precious by-product of belonging to the Vienna analytic group.

When I met Robert Waelder the first time as émigré—he had settled in Philadelphia—he was very disturbed by the cultural difference between Vienna and his new place of activity. He said to me almost in despair: "How can one teach here, where one cannot use a single classical quotation!" By *classical* he meant, of course, Latin or Greek. However, he must have adjusted very well to having to teach without what he at first missed so much, because he was soon widely known as a brilliant teacher of psychoanalysis. He was in great demand as an excellent speaker in scientific meetings because of the superb clarity with which he could speak, even without classical quotations.

SOCIETY MEMBERS WHO GRADUATED FROM THE VIENNA PSYCHOANALYTIC INSTITUTE

Two people who played an important role among the generation of my contemporaries, both for me personally and in the analytic group in general, were Edward and Grete Bibring. I found Edward Bibring an interesting and intellectually superior colleague with whom I would have liked to develop a friendship. But my attempts to come closer to him were unsuccessful, partly, I think, because he was not given to closeness and partly—and this is a subjective feeling—because he resented the ease and facility with which I could present clinical material and organize my presentations. He seemed to have great difficulty in writing. His compulsive character forced him to research a subject so thoroughly that the progress of his scientific production was very slow. In my opinion, he had many more important things to say than his meager literary output shows. Once he expressed his envy of my gift of writing quite openly. After I had presented a case in Wilhelm Reich's seminar, he said: "Sterba, how do you do it that your presentations are always so clear and well put together?" I had no special explanation and told him that I just sit down and write and the organization occurs by itself. He resented my facility for expressing myself in writing whereas he had such difficulty due to his compulsive thoroughness in collecting references and presenting every facet of his subject. A French writer—I have forgotten who it was—once said, "On ne finit jamais une oeuvre, on l'abandonne" (one never finishes a work, one abandons it). Bibring seemed to have had difficulties in abandoning.

Once we made a Sunday outing into the Wachau with the Bibrings and Robert Waelder. The Wachau is a narrow valley through which the Danube flows toward the plain northwest of Vienna. It is famous for its wines, and the southern slopes of the mountains that close in upon it are covered with terraced vineyards. Since in the Wachau there are no industrial plants with ugly smokestacks to disturb the landscape, the valley preserves its romantic, medieval character and it is a favorite area for Sunday outings for the Viennese. The Wachau begins at the Benedictine monastery of Melk, famous for its Baroque church and its bastion overlooking the Danube valley. It ends at Krems, an old medieval city. During this stretch, the mountains narrow the river and its current becomes very swift. The hills and mountains along the Danube are studded with the ruins or still-intact medieval castles and Gothic and Baroque churches.

On our outing, Edward Bibring wore gloves, a not uncommon practice during train rides because the coal used in the steam engines caused a lot of soot to come in through the open windows. I think that only he, among us five, had brought gloves along. However, what struck us as peculiar and significant was that he did not take his gloves off during the whole day, despite the warm weather and some mocking remarks by his travel companions. On another occasion we observed that he entered every little expense in a small black notebook he carried with him.

These are minor but characteristic observations. Edward Bibring was very proud of the *w* in his first name and repeatedly emphasized that his name was "Edward" and not "Eduard," which would be the German spelling of his name, although he came from Czernowitz in the Bucovina. One attitude of his I found irritating. I dislike it in everyone who displays it. It is based on a highly narcissistic involvement with all personal possessions or experiences. Whatever people with this character trait do or possess is, in their own estimation, something very special and unique. If Bibring spoke of a trip of his, or of the acquisition of some possession, he did it in such a way that you had the impression that he thought that his experience or possession was of a higher value or greater importance than yours, even if you possessed the same object or had the same experience. I admit that I found this trait particularly annoying in Bibring, since for some time I had tried to come closer to him. I recognized and appreciated his exceptional honesty, his wide range of interests, and his outstanding qualities as a rigorous theoretician and as an astute clinician and analytic therapist. However, a rivalry existed between us throughout our Vienna years which was beneficial to both of us. We vied with each other over the extent and the quality of our scientific productivity. He seemed to be particularly critical when I published my introduction to the psychoanalytic theory of the libido as well as some of my papers on applied psychoanalysis; some of his criticisms were not unfounded.

Edward Bibring's wife, Grete, was highly intelligent and an excellent analyst. I find it regrettable that she did not put more of her knowledge and experience into writing. Besides her outstanding qualities as a therapist, she had an uncanny political instinct. Helene Deutsch told me once that Grete had such political astuteness.that she not only knew who would be the next upcoming personality of importance but also divined who would come after the next rising personality. She certainly had one great gift: she knew how to make herself the center of attention.

Grete Bibring had a very unfortunate experience. Her dermatologist had given her an anesthetizing injection in her right index finger in order to remove a wart. The adrenalin in the solution caused a severe spasm in the arteries of the finger, and no administration of vasodilating drugs stopped the spasm. The result was gangrene of the fingertip, which was very painful and after some weeks led to the loss of the fingertip. The amazing spectacle was how, with an unbelievable gift for *mise en scène*, Grete managed to become the center of interest and compassion of the whole analytic group during that period. It became *de rigueur* that her colleagues pay her a visit every afternoon between four and six o'clock, when she held circle in her living room like a queen receiving her courtiers. The room was filled with flowers and the coming and going was like the *grand lever* of a person of rank. It was a masterful accomplishment how she turned her unfortunate mishap into an event of central interest to the whole circle.

Heinz Hartmann, the third member of the triumvirate of methodologists of the Vienna Psychoanalytic Society, was a personality vastly different from Robert Waelder and Ernst Kris. What impressed one about him was his coolness and a distinguished distance of Olympian superiority. This made it difficult to listen to his presentations as well as to read his written work. When he presented a paper, one had the feeling that he was disinterested in his audience and had little empathy for their reaction. In fact, the larger the audience, the more he seemed to withdraw from it. This was particularly obvious to me when he read a paper to a large audience at a meeting of the society for medical psychology in Vienna. On this occasion, he walked up and down in front of his listeners while lecturing. When he reached the end of the podium and had to turn back, he made his turn not facing the audience but in the opposite direction, so during the turn he spoke to the blackboard, as if he were not directing his address to his listeners. I personally did not find his aloofness offensive, because I had the feeling that his intellectual superiority and the wealth of his knowledge demanded such respect and—on my part at least—admiration that I found his superior attitude appropriate. The only thing I missed in his work was clinical material; there is hardly any mention made of material from analytic or other clinical cases. I was never close to him personally; someone who was might be able to do a fuller characterization of the great methodologist of our scientific group.

Another lay member of the society who gained world-wide recognition was Edith Buxbaum. Her deep human and psychodynamic understanding of children established very early her reputation as a therapist for children and adolescents. We enjoyed her company on many excursions in the Wienerwald.

Ernst Kris is so well known from his writings and his frequent presentations at national and international meetings that I cannot add much to the characterization of his personality. I considered him a superior person in every respect. He was well versed in many fields of knowledge besides being an expert in the history of art and a brilliant psychoanalytic theoretician and technician. His ideas and concepts always proved fruitful and stimulating. His knowledge of the classical and several modern languages contributed to his vast store of literary knowledge. Next to Freud, Kris and Waelder came closest to the image of the *polyhistor*, as the great scholars of Western culture were called. At the same time, Kris was not an aggressive person, and to my knowledge he was always friendly in his contact with his colleagues. When he criticized my early paper on Gothic art, he did it so tactfully that it was easy for me to accept his remarks and to learn from them. I followed his progress as an analytic therapist from his first reports in the technical seminar at the time when Helene Deutsch conducted it to his later case presentations, and I marveled at the rapid growth of his insight into the unconscious and his technical skill. He was a brilliant star in the Viennese analytic constellation. His verbal facility and clarity of expression contributed considerably to his excellence. I felt his untimely death in 1956 as a deep personal loss, although unfortunately we had little contact with him after our emigration.

It was of great significance for all of us when in the middle of the twenties Marie Bonaparte joined the Viennese group of analysts and became a member of the society. Most of the members had been born and brought up as commoners in the Austro-Hungarian monarchy, and many had served in the army and fought in World War I for "God, Kaiser, and fatherland." In this "fatherland" the aristocracy had played a dominant role. Prince Metternich's sharp distinction between noble and plebeian, well preserved in the monarchy, was expressed in his famous saying: "For me the human being starts at the baron." Although this distinction was considerably diminished when the liberal bourgeoisie rose to power in the 1860s and 1870s, and more so when nobility was abolished, after the destruction of the monarchy the general public still considered members of the aristocracy to be persons of a higher quality than the ordinary citizens. When I rode with the lord of a large estate in Czechoslovakia in his carriage through the fields, some of the older tenant farmers would come running to the carriage to show their reverence by kissing the count's coat sleeve.

Even in Vienna, most people considered a count or prince as somebody of a higher order. They were usually addressed by their former title, such as *Herr Graf* or *Durchlaucht* (serene highness). The early imprinting of respect for members of the aristocracy was not easily eliminated. Officially one should have addressed Princess Marie Bonaparte as *koenigliche Hoheit,* or *altesse royale* (royal highness) if one spoke French to her. But the analysts addressed her with a simple *Prinzessin.* She had the appearance of a regal personality, without putting on any airs. She was tall and her facial features were of natural nobility although she came partly from bourgeois parentage. Her German was fluent, as was her English, although both were spoken with a slight French accent. Editha and I enjoyed it most when she spoke French, which was of the highest quality. She was well educated and had a vast knowledge of Western literature. Her presence at meetings automatically lifted the standard of behavior. Of course, her closeness to the professor and to Anna contributed to her higher status among us.

Although Marie Bonaparte had obviously been educated for her role as a *grande dame du monde,* in the years in Vienna she was a very serious student of psychoanalysis and an industrious research worker. Her bibliography, the high quality of her scientific books and papers, and the sincerity of the revelations she made about herself in her writings give witness to the high standard of her scholarship.

During the congress in Paris in 1938, which we attended as refugees (living temporarily in Switzerland and traveling on passports that were already invalid), Marie Bonaparte gave a garden party at her city palace. Usually she resided at her castle in St. Cloud. The congress took place during a heat wave, and there were no air conditioners in existence yet. Everybody was suffering under the heat, which hardly diminished at night, and there were three hundred guests assembled in the park of the palace. Two valets were occupied solely with the opening of champagne bottles. The delightful bubbling liquid quenched the thirst that everybody felt and it soothed the sorrows and anxieties of those who were already without a home country. In the library of the palace, Yvette Guilbert, the great chanteuse, sang some of her famous songs. Sigmund Freud was a great admirer of Yvette Guilbert. I had heard that before his sickness, Freud always attended her recitals in Vienna. A photograph of her hung on the wall in Freud's study. It carried the handwritten inscription "Au savant l'artiste" (the artist to the sage). When she sang at the Paris congress in 1938 in the library of Marie Bonaparte's palace, she must have been nearly eighty years old. But her power of acting was undiminished and so convincing that she appeared young and beautiful when she sang: "Dites moi que je suis belle" (tell me that I am beautiful). We shared Freud's admiration for her.

Max Schur was a remarkable contemporary of ours. He had been analyzed by Ruth Mack-Brunswick. He was an internist with vast medical knowledge and an excellent medical diagnostician and clinician. In 1928, he replaced Felix Deutsch as Freud's personal physician. In the late twenties he became our family physician and personal friend. He underwent analytic training and joined the society in 1933. His financé and later his wife, Helene, who also had a medical degree, Max, Editha, and I frequently spent our weekends together, on skis in winter and early spring and hiking in the Wienerwald in spring and fall. During summer vacations, the Schurs visited us in our summer home in Gmunden. Later, our children were close in age, which gave us more opportunities for common ties. During these years, Max Schur gravitated more and more from his practice as an internist toward becoming an analyst. When he settled in New York in 1939, he devoted himself to analytic work and writing. Since he was Freud's personal physician, he would have been the best source of information about Freud's physical condition and the different recurrences of his oral cancer, the many operations and painful recoveries. But he never volunteered to tell us anything about Freud's condition and we took this as a cue not to ask him about it. Schur's discretion at that time was absolute and we respected it and held him in high esteem for it.

Max Schur was the only one besides Felix Deutsch in our circle who had a car. It was a Tatra, made in Czechoslovakia. It seated four persons, two of whom had to sit in the rumble seat. Max was a fast driver, and at eighty kilometers per hour the car rattled as if it would fall apart. But we enjoyed the opportunity that Max offered us to reach the Vienna Woods without having to ride on crowded trains or streetcars. Max and Helene Schur became our best friends in the analytic group. They were among those few with whom we were *per Du*, a linguistic sign of closeness.

Among the group of my contemporaries were two who did not quite blend in with the psychoanalytic group as a whole: Ludwig Eidelberg and Edmund Bergler. I believe Eidelberg and Max Schur had been friends or even schoolmates in their home town in the eastern part of the Austro-Hungarian monarchy. I imagine that Schur had motivated Eidelberg to go into training analysis with Ruth Mack-Brunswick. Eidelberg was a highly intelligent, very lively, and witty person, although he did not seem to have acquired the cultural level that was the standard of the analytic group. He was keenly interested in sports events. I remember that he took Editha and me to watch a professional soccer match. This was the first and only time we watched such a group sport event while we lived in Austria. He also favored scientific teamwork with another research analyst. In general, psychoanalytic researchers produced and published individually, since at that time the basic research material, the production of the patient on the couch, excluded the direct participation of a second observer. However, a general survey of the results of analytic work with patients and work applied to other fields permits coauthorship. Otto Rank and Hanns Sachs had published together

Die Bedeutung der Psychoanalyse fuer die Geisteswissenschaften (The significance of psychoanalysis for the mental sciences [New York, 1916]). Ferenczi and Rank coauthored a book called *Entwicklungsziele der Psychoanalyse* (Development of psychoanalysis [Washington, D.C., 1925]). But these were exceptions. Eidelberg seemed to have a proclivity for working with another researcher. He did so first in the neurological field on positional reflexes with Paul Schilder, and on conditioned reflexes with Kestenbaum. In the analytic field he cooperated with Ludwig Jekels and later extensively with Edmund Bergler. Eidelberg impressed me as conceited and endowed with an unpleasant type of narcissism. At times his behavior was rude. I remember that once in a meeting of the Kinderseminar he sat on a sofa next to Princess Marie Bonaparte. In the course of the evening he leaned on her in a sloppy manner and did not disturb his position when the princess tried to move away as far as the armrest of the sofa permitted. Editha and I felt very uncomfortable when we observed his boorishness and the obvious discomfort of the princess. We felt that this was a manifestation of rudeness and insensitivity.

Edmund Bergler became notorious for his fecundity in producing papers. What set him apart from the group was that he spoke with a somewhat coarser Viennese dialect and used less cultivated language than that spoken by most of the members of the society, which was a Viennese version of High German. He was a widely read and a diligent researcher. I always found it amazing that an analyst during his lifetime would be able to find thirty writers with writer's block, about which Bergler published a well-known study in the United States. However, it is meritorious that he established the oral masochism as a common character trait in writers.

Bergler gained a certain reputation in literary circles because of his work on writer's block. Waelder, who was an editor of the German *Imago*, told me a few years ago that in Vienna, the editorial staff of the journal accepted only every third paper by Bergler, whereas in the United States, the journals, in their eagerness to fill their publications, accepted everything he wrote.

I observed a hierarchical structure in the Vienna analytic group. A special group consisted of the analysts who were in closest personal contact with Freud. Of course, Anna Freud would have to be mentioned first, then Marie Bonaparte, then Mrs. Dorothy Tiffany-Burlingham, who had been an analysand of Freud's. Between Mrs. Tiffany-Burlingham and Anna Freud a close friendship developed. Jeanne Lampl de Groot seemed to join the close entourage after she had immigrated to Vienna from Holland in the early thirties. Ruth Mack-Brunswick also belonged to this circle.

The second rank of the hierarchical structure consisted of the older members of the society. Paul Federn had frequent contact with Sigmund Freud due to his position as vice-president. Others in this group were Eduard Hitschmann, Ludwig Jekels, Theodor Reik, Isidor Sadger, Maxim Steiner, Siegfried Bernfeld, Hermann Nunberg, Helene and Felix Deutsch, and Robert Hans Jokl. Some of the older members were not active in the society meetings and we hardly got to know them. Nepallek, though he attended meetings regularly, never participated in scientific or technical discussions. I knew his voice only from his early reports of the finances, which he gave for many years as the treasurer of the society. Friedjung, a pediatrician and a Socialist member of the Vienna city council, appeared very rarely in meetings. Maxim Steiner, a sexologist, was not very active in the society. Most of the very early members had not been analyzed.

To the third rank belonged those who had been analyzed and had joined the society before the institute was established. I remember Edward Bibring, Willy Hoffer, Otto Isakower, Robert Waelder, and Heinz Hartmann as belonging to this subgroup, which was not noticeably distinguished from the members who had graduated from the institute, like Grete Bibring, Eduard Kronengold (Kronold), Editha Sterba, Anny Angel-Katan, Edith Buxbaum, Jenny Pollak-Waelder, and me.

I became very much aware of the distance between the echelons of the hierarchical structure of the Viennese group in the summer of 1930. During summer vacation at our home at Gmunden, I once rode on my bicycle to the nearby Grundlsee, one of the most beautiful alpine lakes, in order to visit a group of colleagues. Siegfried Bernfeld was the only higher-ranking member there. The others I remember were Willy Hoffer, Maedi Olden, the sisters Steffi and Berta Bornstein, guests from Berlin, and, I think,

Edith Buxbaum, Hedwig Schaxel (later Hedwig Hoffer), and Annie Reich. They all spent their summer vacation at the east end of the lake. At the west end, at a distance of not more than two miles, was the vacation place of Freud and his entourage. I was told that there was no communication between the two groups. To Freud's company belonged Mrs. Freud, Anna Freud, Minna Bernays, Princess Marie Bonaparte, Mrs. Tiffany-Burlingham, Ruth Mack-Brunswick, Eva Rosenfeld (the niece of Yvette Guilbert), and the maid, Paula Fichtl. Freud appreciated the devotion to and material help for the cause of some members of his entourage. Only later did I learn that during this summer Freud was severely ill. He could not even attend the funeral of his beloved mother in Vienna; Anna Freud represented the family. The following October he had to undergo another major operation.

About Helene Deutsch and Wilhelm Reich I have told in previous chapters. In this chapter I am writing only about members of the society of whom I have distinct memories. I hope that I have given the reader a vivid enough description of the many and manifold talents and characters that composed the Vienna psychoanalytic community. What they had in common was their humanistic *Bildung*. What tied them together was the common cause, that is, the study and promotion of Freud's work, and the devotion to the extraordinary scientist, humanist, and human being Sigmund Freud.

VII. The Last Years in Vienna

While the Vienna Psychoanalytic Institute grew rapidly in the 1930s, the facilities at the Herzstation became deplorably insufficient. Therefore, in 1935 the Vienna Psychoanalytic Society and the institute decided to establish a permanent home of their own. A suitable location was found in an apartment house, Berggasse 7, two blocks from Freud's apartment. Sigmund Freud's oldest son, Ernst, who was established as an architect in England, was entrusted with the architectural changes and decorative arrangements of the new psychoanalytic center. The results of his work were very satisfactory. The new facilities consisted of a beautiful meeting room that could easily seat fifty persons. The drapes and upholstered chairs were of a pleasant Bordeaux red color. The chairs were well proportioned and comfortable, an agreeable contrast to the hardness of the wooden chairs in our former meeting rooms. There were several treatment rooms, a library, and a kitchen. A couple was engaged to do the cleaning and to prepare refreshments for the coffee break, which was a custom at meetings.

The interior design work was timed so that the opening would take place close to Freud's eightieth birthday, 6 May 1936. A solemn meeting opened the new home of the society and the institute. Ernest Jones was the main speaker. His first sentence betrayed the ambivalence so often noticeable in his behavior: "It is a significant sign of the honorable poverty that the Vienna Psychoanalytic Society, the mother of all others, has suffered, that it took more than thirty years until it found a decent home of its own." I remember that John Riviere presented a paper, as did Karl Landauer, who had come from Frankfort for the occasion. The highlight of the celebration was a paper by Thomas Mann given at the invitation of the Academic Society for Medical Psychology. He presented it in a medium-sized auditorium, the Mittlere Konzerthaussaal, to an audience of approximately seven hundred, including analysts from England, France, Holland, Czechoslovakia, and Hungary. (No one from Germany was present.) It was a most solemn black-tie affair. The title of the paper was "Freud und die Zukunft" (Freud and the future). Mann spoke with beautiful diction and carefully selected emphasis so that the Gestalt of every sentence could be easily grasped. I was deeply impressed and elated that the greatest German writer of the period paid homage to the work of the man to whom I owed so much.

Following Thomas Mann's presentation was a formal dinner at the Hotel Imperial, where the society members were introduced to Mann and shook hands with the great writer. Freud himself was too weak and ailing to appear at any meetings. A few days later, Mann presented his paper to Freud in his summer place in the outskirts of Vienna. Since Freud was then already an international celebrity, the postman and telegram carrier arrived at Freud's place with knapsacks full of congratulatory messages. It was known that one of Freud's favorite flowers was the delicate small variety of anthurium, and on 6 May the Vienna florists were sold out of this plant. To all this influx of messages and gifts from well wishers Freud remarked: "Now I know how the Canadian quintuplets feel, only they were used to it from birth."

Another special society meeting took place around this time. It was scheduled on a Sunday morning. The meeting was devoted to a discussion of Anna Freud's most recent publication, "The Ego and the Mechanisms of Defense," a landmark work. According to my memory, the discussion that took place at that time did not do justice to this work, which became of such importance for the development of ego psychology.

These two events in May of 1936 were the culmination of two decades of my life with the Vienna Psychoanalytic Society. My own contribution to Freud's eightieth birthday was the appearance of the first issue of my *Handwoerterbuch der Psychoanalyse* (Dictionary of psychoanalysis), covering the definitions from *Abulie* (abulia) to part of the term *Angst* (anxiety). Freud acknowledged the dedication by giving me a rarely reproduced photograph with his signature.

From then on, the dark clouds of Nazism threatened Austria more and more and made the existence of all of us increasingly insecure. Felix and Helen Deutsch had already left the sinking ship and had immigrated to the United States in the early thirties. Hermann Nunberg had emigrated a few years earlier. Siegfried Bernfeld had told me one or two years before: "Sterba, remember, when I leave here it is time to move out of Austria. I have a sense for the right time to escape." He left for Italy in 1936 and later settled in San Francisco.

In November 1936, a board meeting of the society was called on a Sunday afternoon. The discussion at the meeting showed Freud's attitude to the Berlin members who had remained in Germany after the takeover by the Nazis. By then I had been appointed by the board as the librarian of the society and as such had become a member of the board. The meeting was to take place at Freud's apartment. Its purpose was to hear a report on the activity of the Berlin group under Hitler's regime. Felix Boehm, the leader of the analysts who had stayed in Germany, had come to Vienna to give this report. When I arrived for the meeting at Berggasse 19, I encountered Boehm at the entrance of Freud's house. (I had previously met him at the International Congress in Luzern in 1934.) Boehm and I walked up the stairs together and I rang the doorbell to Freud's apartment. Paula, the maid, opened the door and let us in. Freud happened to be in the entrance hall. Freud greeted Boehm in his usual friendly manner, while I kept in the background. Then Freud looked at me. Since there was no light on in the hall, it was rather dark, and I thought that Freud might not be able to recognize who I was. So I said, "I am Dr. Sterba." Freud came to me, embraced me, and said to Anna, who had just entered the hall: "What do you think, Anna? Sterba thinks I have lost my memory and I would not recognize him." It was a most moving experience to be greeted so warmly by the great man.

We then entered the room in which the rest of the members were already assembled. I do not remember in which room in Freud's apartment the meeting took place; however, I remember that Freud sat at some distance to my left, and Boehm sat opposite me. Freud opened the meeting by asking Boehm to give his report. My feeling was that it was his conscience that had motivated Boehm to come to Freud to justify what he had done with (or to?) analysis under the Nazi regime. Boehm reported somewhat boastfully that the Berlin Psychoanalytic Institute had been absorbed by the Deutsche Psychotherapeutische Institut, under the directorship of Professor Goehring, a relative of the Reichsmarschall Hermann Goehring. Boehm presented it as a great achievement of his that at this institute psychoanalysis could still be taught on a par with Alfred Adler's individual psychology and C. G. Jung's type of psychology and therapy. Freud interrupted Boehm to ask: "How long do your teaching courses take?" Boehm's answer was "Two years." Then Freud remarked: "Psychoanalysis one can teach for two years, for three years, for four years. But how can you teach Adler for two years? Adler's ideas and technique can be easily learned in two weeks because with Adler there is so little to know." (Adler had simplified the psychic dynamics to the basic complex of "masculine protest" by which he explained all pathological manifestations of neurosis and psychosis. Through oversimplification Adler had reduced the complicated structure of neurosis to a single, easily applicable formula—which explains his great popularity.) Boehm did not have the answer to Freud's question, but in order to emphasize the acceptance of psychoanalysis by the Deutsche Psychotherapeutische Institut, he said that he would gladly invite one of the members of the Vienna society to present a paper to the Berlin Institute. At this point Freud looked at Boehm over his glasses, as was his habit when he spoke to somebody at a certain distance, and asked: "Whom would you invite?" Boehm's quick answer was "Dr. Sterba, for example." I can still in my memory see Freud looking questioningly at me. I said, without hesitation, "I will gladly accept an invitation after one of my Jewish Viennese colleagues has been invited to speak at the Berlin Institute." Boehm remained silent. Freud only smiled, and the subject was not mentioned any more.

Boehm's presentation and behavior left us all with the impression that he had managed to retain analysis at the institute more in name than in substance and that he did this probably by insincerity, maneuvering, and yielding to political pressure. From what Anna Freud said to me at the last meeting of the board (on which I shall report later), I have to assume that Anna and the professor had the same impression as I had. Freud ended the meeting with an admonition to Boehm which I thought was in reality a tactful, indirect condemnation. He said "You may make all kinds of sacrifices, but you are not to make any concessions." But Boehm had obviously made many concessions already. We board members left the meeting with feelings of unhappiness and worry concerning our future.

There was still another society meeting with an important presentation, the full impact of which was delayed by the tumultuous political events of the period. This was a paper delivered by Heinz Hartmann, on "The Ego and Function of Adaptation." In it, Hartmann established the concepts of the autonomous function of the ego, of the conflict-free areas of the ego, and of the neutralization of mental energy. These concepts initiated the phase of analytic theory building that is termed *ego psychology*. Hartmann's concepts dominated the field until recently, when the theoretical and practical interest began to return to the drive-dominated earliest object relationships. As far as I remember, Hartmann's presentation was the last event of major importance in the meetings of the Vienna Psychoanalytic Society.

From January 1938 on, we lived with growing apprehension. The pressure of the Nazi neighbor on Austria increased. We all felt that Austria could not withstand it much longer. The one-thousand-mark duty that the Hitler regime demanded from any German citizen who traveled to Austria had severely damaged the Austrian economy, whose financial situation depended on German tourists and vacationers. Austria has much to offer as a ski and vacation country and is much less expensive than Switzerland. Its ski territories are among the choicest in the Alps. The lovely Moran lakes in upper Austria and Salzburg are of unsurpassed beauty. The lakes in Carinthia and Styria, on the southern slopes of the Alps, provide ideal summer resorts, with bathing beaches surrounded by magnificent landscapes and offering ideal conditions for water sports. Our country was usually inundated by tourists, particularly from Germany. The "1000-Mark Sperre," as the duty for Germans traveling into Austria was called, dried tourism to a trickle.

The underground Nazi movement in Austria, supported

financially by Germany, caused increasing trouble. In 1934, Chancellor Dollfuss had been brutally murdered by Austrian Nazis at the instigation of Hitler. This outrage had temporarily strengthened the loyal population of Austria in its resistance against the Nazi neighbor. But the undermining influence went on, and the increasing number of unemployed could easily be bought for the Nazi cause by money that flowed in from Germany for this purpose. What we learned from German refugees about the mistreatment of Jews by the Nazis caused us to be greatly alarmed for the welfare of Freud in the event that Austria fell victim to the threatening giant neighbor. This concern motivated my close friend Joseph Weinmann, Freud's dentist, and me to appeal to Anna Freud to take precautions for Freud's safety. I think it was late in 1937 that we urged her to have her father leave Austria for a safer country. She told us in no uncertain terms that he would not hear of it and that he did not want to be approached about this matter because he had decided to stay until the end of his days in Vienna, where he had lived and worked all his life.

A year earlier, Editha and I had been invited to settle in the United States. When Editha discussed the matter with Anna Freud, Anna told her that the professor wished to hold the Viennese group together as long as possible. He considered the cohesive existence of the Vienna group important for the continual growth of his science.

Early in February 1938, the Austrian chancellor, Kurt von Schuschnigg, was summoned by Adolf Hitler to Berchtesgaden. Hitler demanded that the chancellor take some well-known Austrian Nazis into his cabinet. Hitler threatened Schuschnigg that if he did not do so, Austria would have to feel the full power of the German Reich. We knew then that Austria was lost. The next day, I went to the American consulate and applied for immigration visas for myself and my family. From then on, the pressure of the German-supported underground Austrian Nazi party was felt more and more intensely. As a last measure, Chancellor Schuschnigg tried to hold a plebiscite; it would have shown that not more than 35 percent of the Austrian population was in favor of the *Anschluss*, the fusion with the German Reich. Hitler counteracted quickly. On the Friday before the Sunday of the plebiscite, which was set for 13 March, the German army marched into Austria. On Saturday, 12 March, Hitler himself came to Vienna. The Vienna Nazis celebrated Hitler's triumphant appearance on the balcony of the Imperial Hotel with frenetic enthusiasm.

For the rest of the Austrian population, the takeover of Austria by the Germans was utterly depressing. The whole city changed overnight. The *Deutsche Wehrmacht*, in the form of tanks and motorized artillery, drove through the main streets, infantry marched in their typical goose step on the streets of the old imperial residence, and hordes of jubilant Austrian Nazis made their presence felt in all parts of Vienna, screaming "Heil Hitler" and "Down with the Jews." The anti-Nazi part of the population was paralyzed by fear and a deep sense of defeat. On Saturday evening, Editha and I took our friends Dr. Josef Weinmann and his wife, Dr. Bertl Weinmann, to the western railroad, where they took a train to Switzerland. It was with a heavy heart that we were left behind. The uncertainty of our future lay oppressively upon us.

A meeting of the board of the society was called for Sunday afternoon, 13 March, at Berggasse 19. The meeting was chaired by Anna Freud. The mood of the members was gloomy and apprehensive. We all recognized that we had to face the end of all activities of the Vienna Society and Institute. After a short discussion, Anna Freud asked each member what he intended to do. One after the other declared his intention to emigrate to another country, preferably England or the United States. When Anna directed this question to me, I felt that the other board members awaited my answer with a certain uneasiness, since I was the only non-Jewish member of the board present. When I declared that I was determined to emigrate at the earliest possibility, my answer was received with noticeable relief and Anna Freud said: "We expected that you would not play the role in Vienna that Felix Boehm plays in Berlin." Anna then left the room to ask the professor to join the meeting. When Freud entered, Anna told him of the board's decision that the seat of the Vienna Psychoanalytic Society would be wherever Freud would settle and of the intention of its members to leave Austria. When we got up from our chairs to take leave, Freud remarked: "After the destruction of the

Temple in Jerusalem by Titus, Rabbi Jochanan ben Sakkai asked for permission to open a school at Jabneh for the study of the Torah.* We are going to do the same. We are, after all, used to persecution by our history, tradition, and some of us by personal experience, with one exception." He pointed at me and smiled benevolently. The gesture of his hand was done with such charm and in a manner that it made me more included than excluded. We shook hands with Freud at leave taking. We all left this last official meeting of the society with a heavy heart. It was the last time that I saw Sigmund Freud.†

During a sleepless night from Monday to Tuesday, I decided that we would have to leave Austria as quickly as possible and try to establish ourselves in another country. Editha somewhat reluctantly agreed; the decision was more difficult for her because she was so very much attached to her family estate in Gmunden. However, when she visited some Jewish friends in our neighborhood the next morning, she was witness to a scene that convinced her that it was impossible for us to remain in Austria. While she was visiting, storm troopers came to the apartment of our friends and confiscated the passport of the lady's father. They treated the ailing old gentleman with utter rudeness and lack of any consideration for his age and frailty. Editha was outraged at this incident and knew then that we had to leave the country.

On Tuesday, we were busy with preparations for our departure for Switzerland. Tuesday afternoon we went to Berggasse 19 to inform Anna Freud of our plans. She could not see us. Dr. Julia Deming spoke to us as her representative and said she would communicate our decision to Anna. There followed a night of hasty packing and difficult decisions about what to take among our most important personal possessions. We did not expect that we would ever see our books, our artworks, and our furniture again. Our housekeeper, a simple but very devoted woman who had been with us for ten years and had been a loving and caring

---

*This remark may also be found in Freud's *Moses and Monotheism, Standard Edition*, vol. 23, p. 115.

†When Ernest Jones was working on the third volume of his biography of Freud (New York: Basic Books, 1959), I sent him my report on this last meeting of the board, which he took verbatim and included in the third volume of his biography, on page 221.

second mother to our two daughters, then one and a half and five years old, decided to leave Vienna with us. She had two sisters living in New England and our intention was to immigrate with her to the United States. Her willingness to leave with us made the last preparations for departure and the total emigration process considerably easier. I had to inform my patients by telephone of my decision; there was no time to see them because I expected that the frontiers would soon be closed and then one would have to secure a special permit to leave. Since the new Nazi authorities had immediately annulled the medical licenses of two thousand Jewish physicians in Vienna, I doubted that as an Aryan doctor I would be able to obtain a permit to leave the country with my family. I had to take the risk of being kept back at the frontier. A Dutch patient of mine, a girl in her twenties, suggested that I go with her to the Dutch consulate. There she told the consul that her parents wanted her to return to Holland because the political turmoil in Austria was so upsetting that it aggravated her nervous condition. It was supposed to be the wish of her parents that I, as her physician, accompany her on her trip home. The consul immediately issued her a certificate to this effect, which was very useful when I crossed the Austrian-Swiss border. Editha and I had decided that we should take different routes so that it would not be too obvious that we were fleeing. I would take a direct train to Switzerland on Wednesday, 16 March, at 2:00 P.M. Editha, the children, and our housekeeper would take the evening express to Italy. Fortunately, there were still two compartments obtainable in the sleeping car to Venice-Milan.

My time was running short. After our visit to the Dutch consulate, I rushed to the university to talk to Professor Poetzl, head of the Department of Psychiatry, who had succeeded Wagner von Jauregg. He was a member of the Vienna Psychoanalytic Society, but had never participated in any of the society's activities. A few months earlier, I had applied to Poetzl for an assistant professorship in the Department of Psychiatry. I had to accompany my application with my most important personal documents, the certificate of birth, the marriage certificate, and the certificate of Austrian citizenship. It was essential to obtain these documents and take them along on my emigration. When I entered Poetzl's office, he greeted me with outstretched right arm and "Heil Hitler." I answered with only a simple "Guten Tag, Herr Professor." He ignored my defiant response and said: "Now I can make you an *associate* professor right away" (although I had only applied for an assistant professorship). I replied: "I am sorry, but I have decided to leave Austria today and I came to ask you for my personal documents." He found them quickly and handed them to me. No further word was spoken. I thanked him perfunctorily and left.

I had just enough time to rush home for my luggage, then say farewell to my wife and children and the housekeeper, hoping that we would see each other again in two days in Basel, Switzerland. When I arrived the next morning at the border station of Buchs, St. Gallen, I had no difficulty crossing the frontier. Two SS men came into the compartment and I showed them the certificate of the Dutch consulate. I asked them to be gentle with my very disturbed patient. We willingly opened our luggage for inspection. They went through it superficially and left without further questions. From what I could observe, nobody on the train was held back by the SS men. The train rolled out of the frontier station, we crossed the Rhine River, and we arrived in Switzerland with a sigh of tremendous relief. Only then did everyone in the compartment become fully aware of the depression and apprehension that the four days under the Nazi regime had instilled in our minds. I arrived in Basel in the early morning of 17 March.

Even before my family arrived in Basel the following evening, I paid a visit to Dr. Philipp Sarasin, a Basel psychoanalyst and longstanding friend of ours. Sarasin had been in analysis with Sigmund Freud during the early twenties, when we had met him in Vienna. Later we had renewed our contact at international meetings and at occasional visits in Basel. At the time of my arrival in Basel in March 1938, he was president of the Swiss Psychoanalytic Society. We discussed how we could notify our Viennese colleagues that the frontier to Switzerland was still open and that nobody was being prevented from leaving Austria. We decided that the best way would be to invite all Vienna analysts by telegram to a fictitious scientific meeting that would take place in a few days in Zurich. Philipp Sarasin sent the wires immediately. We intended through this ruse to inform our colleagues that the border was open, without taking the chance of speaking openly to them by telephone or in writing. But our Jewish colleagues in Vienna were already too terrorized to take the risk and escape quickly. It took some agonizing months under the Nazi harassment until they obtained the official permits to emigrate, and they then had to leave all of their possessions behind.

Editha, the children, and our housekeeper had no difficulty crossing the frontier on the train to Milan, where they stayed overnight at a hotel. The next day they arrived by train in Basel and we were happily united. Fortunately, we were not financially destitute. I had asked the father of a young Canadian patient of mine to send the fee for the treatment to a friend in Switzerland, who deposited it in a bank. At that time there was a saying going around in Austria: "Money alone does not make you happy. You have to have it in Switzerland." I was glad that I had taken this precaution, by which I had accumulated the fee for three years of analytic treatment in a Swiss bank.

With the help of a lawyer who was a distant relative, we obtained a temporary permit to remain in Basel. We had chosen Basel because relatives of Editha's sister-in-law owned a beautiful house where we could stay temporarily. From Basel I went to the American consulate in Zurich and tried to obtain an American visa for the family. The consul (his appropriate name was Frost) told me that I could obtain visas for myself, the children, and the housekeeper within a few months, but for Editha, who had been born in Budapest (although she was an Austrian citizen), the waiting period would be thirteen years. The Hungarian quota was very small. I accepted Consul Frost's verdict and let myself be discouraged from trying to immigrate to the United States. The consul had, in fact, misled me with this information, which contradicted a regulation that the wife should fall under the quota of the husband's nationality.

I then wrote to Ernest Jones and asked him if he could procure an immigration visa to England for me and my family. His answer was a heavy blow to us. He wrote that he would do nothing to help me get a permit. In fact, he said that I would be the last one who would get any assistance from the International Psychoanalytic Association, of which he was then president, because "you should have stayed in Vienna together with August Aichhorn as a memory of psychoanalysis for a happier future."

Before I answered Jones's letter, I asked a Swiss friend, also a distant relative, to travel to Vienna and contact Anna Freud and ask her to confirm that when I had declared my intention to leave Austria at the earliest opportunity, my decision had found the full approval of the executive board of the Vienna Society and of Sigmund Freud. The friend returned within a few days with the answer. Anna Freud and Princess Marie Bonaparte had told my friend that they both, along with the professor, fully consented to my leaving Austria. I then sent a terse letter to Ernest Jones, informing him of the message I had received from Vienna.

Phillip Sarasin, Editha, and I were glad to learn from my friend that the Freud family was unharmed though under surveillance by the Nazi authorities. But from there on the contact with the Freud family was sparse, and we were greatly relieved when Sarasin received news from Anna Freud that the exit permit was finally granted by the Nazi authorities. This was the result of the concerted influence of many personalities in highest political position in four countries who put pressure on the Nazi authorities to leave Freud and his family unharmed and to give them permission to leave Austria. Jones motivated the Home Office in England; Marie Bonaparte used all the political pull that her husband, the uncle of the king of Greece, exerted; W. C. Bullit, the American ambassador to France, exerted pressure via his connection with F. D. Roosevelt; Mussolini was active due to the influence of Edoardo Weiss in Rome. In addition, Marie Bonaparte paid a considerable ransom to have Freud's art treasures released from the greedy hands of the Nazis. On 6 June 1938, Freud and his family arrived in London.

In the meantime, I had received a special delivery letter from Dr. Mueller-Braunschweig, the Berlin analyst who had come to Vienna to make the Vienna Society and Institute a part of the German Psychotherapeutic Association and the Berlin Institute. The letter was sent from Vienna and reads in translation:

Mueller-Braunschweig
at present Vienna, IX. Berggasse 7   Vienna, IX.
(Psycho-Publishing House)   Berggasse 7
4/5/38

Esteemed Dr. Sterba,
    I would like to inform you briefly about the local

events. After the resignation(!) of the Jewish members, the Vienna Psychoanalytic Society has been absorbed by the German Psychoanalytic Society. The next task is to construct out of Berggasse 7 an institute that, like the one in Berlin, permits the different psychotherapeutic schools to work on a basis of equality. In this way, the possibility of survival and work is also secured for analysis. For this we urgently need the full cooperation and assistance of the few Aryan members of the Vienna Psychoanalytic Society. Therefore, I would be very much obliged to you, if I, as the representative of the German Psychoanalytic Society as well as of the German Institute for Psychological Research and Psychotherapy, to which the former is subordinate, could have an extensive personal talk with you. In the first place, I would like to establish immediately a schedule of lectures for the S.S. [probably "summer semester"] 1938. As a member of the German Psychoanalytic Society, you will— if there are no special reasons against this—without further ado, become a member also of the German Institute and in this way would be recognized as a psychotherapist in Germany.

With collegial greetings and HEIL HITLER!
yours,
Dr. Carl Mueller-Braunschweig

P.S. I will stay here approximately two more weeks and would like to establish everything as far as possible.

The letter was handwritten. When I later sent it to Anna Freud, she pointed out that the words "with collegial greetings" and were obviously added later to the "Heil Hitler," which was written in much larger script. (I translate the German *kollegial* as "collegial," since it means from one colleague to another.)

I answered Mueller-Braunschweig that I had no intention of returning to Vienna. But I then understood why Jones was so angry that I had left. He thought that the Psychoanalytic Institute should have been taken over by a non-Jewish physician and member of the society and I was the only one with such qualities. Jones had arrived in Vienna from London a few days after I had left. His intention was to rescue Freud and his family and, while he was there, to assist the Vienna Society after the Anschluss. He was indignant that I had not been there.

In his biography of Freud, Jones quotes his own exclamation

when he learned of my absence: "Oy, our shabbes goy is gone." (*Shabbes goy* is the non-Jewish servant of an orthodox household who has to turn the lights on or off and do other household chores, which Jews are forbidden by Talmudic law to perform on the Sabbath.) I learned only from Helene Deutsch's book *Confrontations with Myself,* published in 1973, why Jones was so irate at my absence when he came to Vienna to rescue Freud. Deutsch writes: "In the period before the war, Ernest Jones had conceived of a plan to transfer the whole Vienna Psychoanalytic Society to England. According to his concept, Richard Sterba, who was not Jewish, and therefore in no danger from the Nazis, should have remained in Vienna to represent the Society. Jones' plan came to nought when most of the members, for personal reasons, decided to emigrate to America instead of England." It is interesting that I was never informed about Jones' plan.

After I sent Jones my own sharply expressed response, telling him that I had left with the express consent of Freud and Anna, he wrote me a polite letter inviting me to London for lunch. I accepted the invitation, even though the trip was risky since my Austrian passport was no longer valid. In Brussels I was pulled out of my sleeping compartment in the middle of the night and interrogated by the Belgian police, who suspected me of being a Communist. I had a hard time convincing them of my political innocence. They set me free just in time to continue my trip on the same train.

I had lunch with Jones in his study. I remember his enormous writing desk covered with books and papers. The lunch was brought in during our visit: it consisted of mutton chops and tomatoes. We shoved some of the books aside and ate seated at the desk. He praised my English and advised me to apply for a visa to South Africa, because there was a need for an experienced teaching and training analyst in Johannesburg, where an analyst named Dr. Wolf wanted to establish an analytic training center. Jones suggested that he would write to Dr. Wolf and ask him to procure our immigration visas to South Africa. When I left after lunch, Jones gave me the book *The King's English* as a present.

I had a short visit with Anna Freud in London. The professor was still recovering from the harassing time in Nazi Vienna and the strenuous journey to Paris and London. Anna agreed with

Jones's advice to try to go to South Africa.

After my return to Switzerland, I went to the South African consulate in Geneva and applied for visas. I wrote to Dr. Wolf and informed him that, at the advice of Ernest Jones, I had applied for immigration visas to South Africa. His answer was a telegram inviting Editha and me to meet him at a certain date in September in Paris. We accepted the invitation and had lunch with Dr. Wolf at the famous restaurant Rôtisserie de la Reine Pedoque. He expressed satisfaction with our willingness to come to Johannesburg and establish with him a psychoanalytic training center there. He assured us that his influence with the governmental authorities would make it certain that our immigration visas would be granted. Editha and I did not develop confidence in the reliability of Dr. Wolf's assurance and we were not surprised that a few weeks later we received written information from Pretoria that our application was rejected. We were not unhappy that we could not go to South Africa, which was so far away from the countries in which our friends had settled. Almost all Viennese analysts and friends had by then settled in England or the United States. We were still stranded in Switzerland, pressured by the Swiss authorities to leave the country. Our only possibility left was to continue, or, rather, renew, our efforts to obtain visas for the United States.

I wrote to a former American patient of mine, whose daughter had been in treatment with Editha, asking if she could give us an affidavit of support, which was needed for an immigration visa.[*] My patient answered that she had already given all of the affidavits that her financial status permitted, but she told an acquaintance of hers about our being stranded in Switzerland. This lady was Laura Z. Hobson, the well-known author of a series of widely read novels, among them *Gentlemen's Agreement*. Hobson immediately got to work on our visas. She gave the necessary affidavits and tirelessly fought the objections of the American consul in Zurich, who threw up one roadblock after the other

---

[*]When the mother, my patient, left for the United States, a year before the Anschluss, her daughter, who was autistic, was boarded with Bruno Bettelheim and his wife. I believe that it was this experience with the girl that contributed to Bettelheim's interest in autistic children.

in order to refuse us the visas; this was in accord with the prevailing policy of the U.S. State Department, which wanted to keep the influx of refugees to a minimum.

We had to wait for six months for the American visas. The Swiss authorities constantly threatened to send us back to Austria, since we were neither Jewish nor political refugees and therefore officially had no right to ask for asylum. It was an agonizing time of fighting for a series of short prolongations of our temporary permit to stay in Switzerland. In order not to overextend the hospitality of our Swiss relatives, we had rented a villa in Ascona, on Lago Maggiore, in the southern canton of Switzerland called the Ticino. The villa was situated above the lake that extends toward the south into Italy. It was here in this idyllic setting that we lived for six months, until the end of January 1939. This was financially possible because six of the foreign patients we had treated in Vienna joined us in Ascona in order to continue their treatment; three were Dutch, two Swiss, one French. The villa was large enough that we could house a series of Viennese friends who, after they had obtained exit permits, were on their way to England or America. They stayed for a few weeks with us and could recover there from the harassment by the Nazis. To our regret, we could not fully enjoy the unsurpassed beauty of the Ticino due to the painful uncertainty of our future.

When our U.S. visas were finally granted, in late January 1939, the American consulate demanded that we obtain valid passports. This meant that I had to apply for them at the German consulate in Lugano. When I appeared before the consul, he was very inquisitive and seemed reluctant to issue them. He asked me why I needed the passports and why I was leaving the German Reich now that it was coming to glory. Then I used a trick. I told him that I was sure that the authorities in Berlin would not approve of his hesitation to issue a German passport for me and my family. I did not directly answer his question but I made him assume that I was on a secret mission. We got our passports the next day.

A few days later, before we left for the United States but after we had our passports and American visas, I gave a violin-piano recital with a Jewish pianist in Ascona for the benefit of Jewish refugee children.

We left for America at the end of January and landed after an extremely stormy crossing on the *Normandie* in New York on 2 February. After a short stay in New York and Chicago, we decided to make our home in Detroit, where we had been invited to teach and train by Dr. Leo Bartemeier, a member of the Chicago Psychoanalytic Society who lived and worked in Detroit. Four of our patients followed us there. A group of Detroit psychiatrists were then commuting for their training at the Chicago Institute. When we settled in Detroit, they were able to complete their training in Detroit. Dr. Fritz Redl, a former analysand of mine, and Dr. John Dorsey, whom we had befriended in Vienna, also helped us to settle in Detroit. Dr. Bartemeier and his wife, Bess, made all efforts to make our resettlement easy and supported us in a most altruistic way.

After receiving the visas to the United States, while still in Switzerland, I wrote to Freud in London to inform him of our immigration plans and to ask his permission to use his preface to my dictionary for an English edition that I intended to take up again. Three days later, I received the following answer, written in longhand:

Lieber Dr. Sterba,

Meine herzlichsten Wuensche fuer Wanderung und Ankunft. Bedienen Sie sich meiner Vorrede nach Bedarf.

Ihr getreuer Freud

My translation is, "My heartfelt wishes for"—and here I get stuck, for I cannot find the proper translation for *Wanderung und Ankunft*. A literal translation would be "migration and arrival," but these words are too prosaic. The English words do not reflect the higher plane of the Goethean style and the flowing line of poetic sound which the German words carry. Even in these two words, the lofty style of Freud, modeled after the greatest German writer, found its expression. Freud continued in his note to me: "Use my preface as you see fit. Your faithful Freud."

Nine months later, 1 October 1939, Sigmund Freud died.

I hope that my eyewitness report illustrates the impact that the great figure of Freud had on all of us in Vienna in the twenties and thirties. It was Freud's courage in the search for truth regardless of the consequences that was imparted to the members of the Vienna analytic community during the time I belonged to it. His effect on all of us gave the group the significance in the history of the analytic movement which the Dutch analyst P. J. van der Leeuw attributes to it when he says: "There has never been such a group. Without them, the preservation, continuation and further growth of Freud's work can scarcely be imagined."

The reader will have become aware of the deep affection that ties me to the man to whose cause I have devoted my life's work. Goethe, whom Freud admired and to whom he owed so much, explained in one sentence how unavoidable a deep emotional tie is to a great man with whom one has had the good fortune to have contact. He said: "Gegen grosse Vorzuege eines anderen gibt es keine Rettungsmittel als die Liebe" (when confronted with the great superiority of another person, there is no other means of salvation but love).

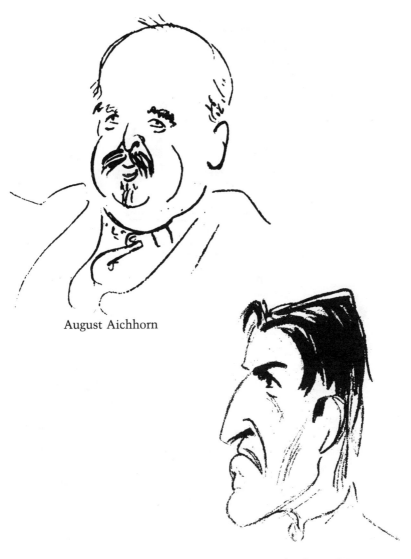

August Aichhorn

Sigfried Bernfeld

The caricatures on this and the following pages were drawn at the International Congress in Salzburg in 1924 by Olga Székely Kovacs and Robert Beréney and were published in *Karikaturen* (Leipzig: Internationaler Psychoanalytischer Verlag, 1924).

Felix Boehm

Felix Deutsch

Helene Deutsch

Paul Federn

Eduard Hitschmann

Sandor Ferenczi

Wilhelm Hoffer

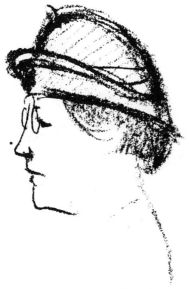

Hermine Hug-Hellmuth

Ludwig Jekels

Robert Jokl

Ernest Jones

Hermann Nunberg

Wilhelm Reich

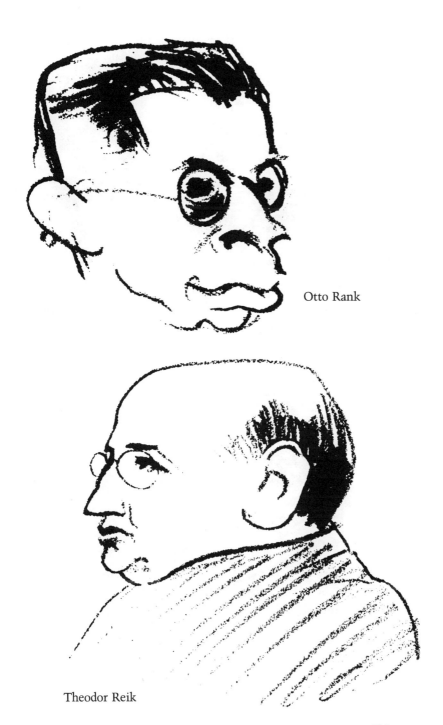

Otto Rank

Theodor Reik

Paul Schilder

A. J. Storfer

Alfred Winterstein

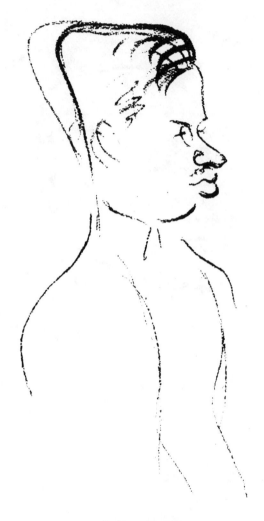

Robert Waelder

A native of Vienna, Richard F. Sterba received his M.D. degree from the University of Vienna Medical School in 1923. He was a member of the first class to receive psychoanalytic training at the Vienna Psychoanalytic Institute and was a training analyst there for ten years. Since his arrival in Detroit in 1939, he has been a practicing psychoanalyst. He has been affiliated with international, national, and state psychoanalytic societies.

Dr. Sterba is the coauthor of *Libido Theory* (1942) and *Beethoven and His Nephew* (1954). He has published extensively in the field of theoretical, clinical, and applied psychoanalysis.

The manuscript was edited by Wendy Harris and Doreen Broder. The book was designed by Jim Billingsley. The typeface for the text and display is Trump Medieval.

The text is printed on Warren's Olde Style Wove, and the book is bound in Holliston Mills' Roxite over binder's boards. Manufactured in the United States of America.